Book Publishing for Authors:

How to Write, Publish and Market Your Book to a #1 Bestseller in the Next 90 Days

By

Paul G. Brodie

Book Publishing for Authors: How to Write, Publish and Market Your Book to a #1 Bestseller in the Next 90 Days

Copyright @ 2017 by Paul G. Brodie

Editing by Devin Rene Mooneyham

All rights reserved in all media. No part of this book may be used or reproduced without written permission, except in the case of brief questions embodied in critical articles and reviews.

The moral right of Paul G. Brodie as the author of this work has been asserted by him in accordance with the Copyright, Designs, and Patents Act of 1988.

Published in the United States by BrodieEDU Publishing, 2017.

Disclaimer

The following viewpoints in this book are those of Paul Brodie. These views are based on his personal experience over the past forty-two years on the planet Earth, especially while living in the great state of Texas.

The intention of this book is to share his stories of both success and struggles with book publishing and what has worked for *him* through this journey.

All attempts have been made to verify the information provided by this publication. Neither the author nor the publisher assumes any responsibility for errors, omissions, or contrary interpretations of the subject matter herein.

This book is for entertainment purposes only. The views expressed are those of the author alone and should not be taken as expert instruction or commands. The reader is responsible for his or her future action. This book makes no guarantees of future income. However, by following the steps that are listed in this book the odds of increased revenue streams for your future book launches have a much higher probability.

Neither the author nor the publisher assume any responsibility or liability on the behalf of the purchaser or reader of these materials.

The views expressed are based on his personal experiences within the corporate world, education, and everyday life.

This book is dedicated to my mom, Barbara "Mama" Brodie. Without her support and motivation (and incredible cooking) I would literally not be here today.

I am also dedicating this book to my coaching clients and the student authors (past graduates, present and future students) in my Book Publishing for Authors Implementation Program. You have all gone above and beyond chasing your dreams to become bestselling authors and I am proud to be able to help you accomplish your dreams.

Table of Contents

Free Training

Editorial Reviews

Foreword by Mimi Emmanuel

Foreword by Scott Allan

Foreword by Lise Cartwright

Introduction

Free Audiobook Offer

Chapter 1 The Journey Begins

Chapter 2 Advice from Bestselling Authors

Chapter 3 Why Are You Writing Your Book?

Chapter 4 Idea Topics for Your Book

Chapter 5 Choosing Your Book Title

Chapter 6 Outlining Your Book

Chapter 7 Writing Your Book

Chapter 8 Editing Your Book

Chapter 9 Formatting Your Book to Kindle

Chapter 10 Choosing Your Book Cover

Chapter 11 Creating Your Book Description

Chapter 12 Uploading Your Book and Kindle Direct Publishing

Chapter 13 Getting Reviews

Chapter 14 Free Launch Strategy

Chapter 15 Paid Strategy at 99 Cents

Chapter 16 Recording Your Audiobook

Chapter 17 Converting Your Book to Paperback

Chapter 18 How to Build Your Audience

Chapter 19 Lead Magnets

Chapter 20 Back-End Products

Chapter 21 Revenue Streams

Chapter 22 Summary: The Book Publishing Journey

More Books by Paul

About the Author

Testimonials

Acknowledgments

Contact Information

Feedback Request

Free Training

Are you looking to publish and market your book to a #1 bestseller in the next 90 days?

I invite you to watch my Get Published Training.

If you are looking to write your own book on travel, business, self-help, or anything else related to non-fiction, this webinar is for you.

If you are writing fiction and children's books, this webinar is for you.

Entrepreneurs, the benefits of writing and publishing a book is an ideal way to build your business. Having a book will help you become an authority in your specific area of expertise.

This is what you will learn on this Free Online Workshop:

- How to turn your book into multiple revenue streams
- How to get your draft turned into an eye-catching book that will help increase sales and attract clients for your speaking, coaching, and online courses
- How to market your book including several promo companies that I will share on the training that are used for every book launch

WARNING: The Webinar is only available for a limited time.

Go to www.BrodieEDU.com and click on the Free Webinar tab to sign up today

Editorial Reviews

"What makes this book different than the other self-publishing how-to books is the author's ability to explain complex ideas and strategies in a simple, easy way that you can use right away. Highly recommended!"

Dr. Michael Unks, Multi-time Bestselling Author of books including Become the Ace, Awesome in Hours, and The Gym of Life

"I enjoyed reading Book Publishing for Authors and working through the material and watching the free online training. Paul is a master in making the complex simple. I couldn't be happier with the results."

Mimi Emmanuel, Multi-time Bestselling Author of books including Live Your Best Life by Writing Your Own Eulogy, My Story of Survival, and God Healed Me

"Paul helps to make the road to writing a book easier and without the bumps that so many first-time authors needlessly go through."

Barry Watson, Multi-time Bestselling Author of books including Sell With Confidence, Relationship Rehab, and Rock Solid Relationship

"If you're a writer dreaming of seeing your own books being snatched off the (virtual and real) shelves – this book is for you."

Joanna Jast, Multi-time Bestselling Author of books including Laser-Sharp Focus and Hack Your Habits

"Paul Brodie breaks down the publishing journey really well in this book. A great read for people that are just getting started and want to become successful authors. Read this book and you'll save yourself a ton of time and energy by doing things right the first time."

Tyler Wagner, Multi-time Bestselling Author of books including Conference Crushing, The Better Business Book, and How to Network at Networking Events

"Along with personal examples and experiences, Paul Brodie has put together a resource that every aspiring author should have."

Dustin Heiner, Multi-time Bestselling Author of books including Successfully Unemployed, How to Quit Your Job with Passive Income, and How to Quit Your Job with Rental Properties

"Paul Brodie has taken the complex subject of self-publishing and broken it down into a simple, easy-to-follow system that everyone can adapt to. Follow this course and, with a confident coach to guide you, you will turn your book idea into a bestseller within just a few months."

Scott Allan, Multi-time Bestselling Author of books including Rejection Reset, Do It Scared, and Relaunch Your Life

"This step-by-step guide is perfect if you're about to publish your first book, and it's full of marketing tips for more seasoned authors, too. Brodie provides the foundation, now it's time to follow the steps and launch your book into the world."

Courtney Kenney, Multi-time Bestselling Author of books including Creating Space to Thrive, Layoff Reboot, and 100 Awesome Ideas for Authors

Foreword by Mimi Emmanuel

I am thrilled to write a foreword for Paul Brodie's *Book Publishing for Authors*.

After I published my first book in 2015, I came across Paul's *Book Publishing for Beginners* and loved the flavor of it. This is when I reached out to Paul and he responded in such a genuine and helpful manner that I have been a fan ever since. We are both part of a wonderful author group on Facebook and because of this I have gotten to know Paul and his work quite well.

I have lapped up whatever Paul has given me and he has been a massive help with my book launches. My book, *The Holy Grail of Book Launching* was published in 2016 and became a tremendous success, listing #1 bestseller in 20 categories, not in a small part due to Paul's support with my launch.

I have been privileged to follow The *Book Publishing for Authors Implementation Program* and even after publishing five books, still gained many new insights, and tweaked things here and there after listening to Paul's expert advice. I noticed measurable improvement in sales after rewriting my book description whilst going through the program. Needless to say, I like Paul's Program a lot. There are so many courses and programs available on book publishing nowadays, but where Paul shines is in the experience he brings to the table; with NINE #1 bestsellers to his name.

Not only that, but in addition to being a bestselling author, Paul is an experienced and recognized motivational and inspirational writer and lecturer. This power combo ensures that Paul's readers benefit hugely from his expertise in multiple areas. Paul's multiple talents and work history, combined with his engaging writing style and genuine desire to help others is what sets him apart from the pack and makes him a leader in the field of Self-Publishing.

What I love about Paul is that he shares all his knowledge freely. He does not hold anything back. Once you have read his books and followed his *Book Publishing for Authors Implementation Program* you will have access to the same resources and professionals that helped Paul become a very successful writer.

I love that! Paul's generosity and genuine care shines through in all his books and makes it a joy to read whatever he wants to share.

We all know that our story creates a legacy. I am so grateful that Paul is helping me make mine the best it can be.

I am delighted that Paul once more has decided to share his masterful skills and cannot recommend anything he cares to produce highly enough.

If you are serious about becoming a published bestselling author, I suggest you make sure that *Book Publishing for Authors* becomes a staple in your library, and Paul's *Book Publishing for Authors Implementation Program* your go-to for anything to do with publishing your story.

Paul is very quiet about this, but I know that somewhere, somehow, he gained a Master's degree in 'Making the Complex Simple.'

I know you will enjoy Paul's material, and if the success of Paul's own books, and my book *The Holy Grail of Book Launching*, are anything to go by, you will also get excellent results by following his advice.

I wish for all Paul's readers who aspire to be an author, to follow in his footsteps and be as hugely successful as Paul has become.

Mimi Emmanuel

#1 Bestselling author in 45 categories

www.amazon.com/author/mimiemmanuel

www.mimiemmanuel.com

Foreword by Scott Allan

The writing journey from dreamer to published author started for me about three years ago. Like many people, I had longed to write a book, but I did not know where to begin. I took a few courses, read some books on self-publishing and how to structure a novel, and after three years and at a cost of around $3000.00, I managed to launch my first book on Amazon.

After hitting that publish button, I waited for the sales to come rolling in. And waited.

I ended up selling seven copies.

Frustrated and broke, I needed to know the secret others were using to get their books out there faster. So I did some more research, talked to people in the business, and as it turns out, the successful authors that were making it had a system down. They were publishing every 3 months [not 3 years], and selling hundreds of books during launch week. They were not just marketing to their friends or family but were building an actual business from their books. These authors were getting reviews, had good-looking covers, and were making a living in the self-publishing industry.

So, what was this magic formula?

As it turns out, the 'system' is not as complicated as I had thought. You are going to learn about it in Paul's book.

You might be one of these people with an idea for a book, but you aren't sure where to begin. You might have your own business and you want your book to take it to the next level. Or, becoming a bestselling author is one of your bucket list items that you absolutely need to achieve. You could already be a published author with multiple titles but you need support with the marketing side of the business.

Whatever your goal is, you have arrived in the right place to make it happen. Writing a book and launching it to the world is an exciting venture. You can create a new business, multiple income streams, and work from home or travel the globe. I have seen it work so I know it is possible.

As Walt Disney said, "All our **dreams can come true**, if we have the courage to pursue them."

We Are Not Alone

If there is one thing I learned on this book writing journey it is this: You don't have to do it alone.

As I found out in those earlier days, doing it alone and without a formula is the hard way. If there was a way to get your book written in less than 90 days, and launch it to bestseller status, wouldn't you want to try it out? That is what I did. I started to learn from the best and, when you have a process to work with, it takes out all the guess work. You can finally lose your self-doubt overnight and put your fears to rest.

The system that Paul has put together is a proven formula. I have been using it myself for the past 2 years to launch multiple books on Amazon. What I once thought an impossible goal is now a living reality. You do not have to drift aimlessly, feeling lost and confused wondering if you are heading in the right direction. With the right support and guidance, your 'big idea' can be turned into a bestselling novel in a matter of months.

When I first started out writing, there were not that many systems out there, so it was like flying blind most of the time. I tried this and I experimented with that. I figured out what worked and what didn't. As it turns out, many of the writing and publishing tactics I was using now appear in this book.

Paul's book is your all-to-guide for figuring out your topic, getting crystal clear on why you are writing this book, and navigating through Amazon's platform to launch your dreams. With the tools and guidance, you have access to here, you will get your book written faster and your dream of becoming published will become a reality sooner than you think.

I invite you on this publishing journey to bring your craft to the world and share your message through your story and your gift. The system you are about to learn works and has helped thousands of authors to succeed.

I am confident this self-publishing process will work for you, too. You can make it happen if you decide, commit and take action.

I wish you all the best in your ventures,

Scott Allan

Scott Allan is the #1 bestselling author of Do It Scared, Rejection Reset, *and* Relaunch Your Life. *His mission is to help people overcome their self-defeating behaviors, deal with rejection and build an empowering, freedom-based lifestyle. With a deep passion for teaching, building life skills, and inspiring others to take charge of their lives, he is committed to a path of constant and never-ending self-improvement.*

You can find out more by visiting his blog at http://www.scottallanauthor.com

Foreword by Lise Cartwright

Self-publishing your own book might seem easy enough.

All you need is a Microsoft Word document with your chapter headings, a table of contents, and your book cover. You're good to go…

Until you try to publish your book.

When I first published my first book, questions like, "What format do I need my Kindle book in?" or "Do I need to publish a paperback book at all?" started coming up. Not to mention, which platforms to publish on...

I often say to my coaching students that writing a book is the easy part, and there's a reason that rings true.

It wasn't until I started the publishing process that I learned that there are key things you need to do BEFORE you hit publish, like choose a great book title, or that you need different types of book covers depending on the platform you're publishing on.

Publishing my first book remains one of my greatest achievements.

Imagine receiving a small cardboard box in the mail. All you see is a plain white address label with your name on it and the black Amazon logo... You've been waiting for it, but you're nervous to open it, knowing that in your hands you hold what could be the start of an amazing journey.

You rip open the box and see, for the very first time, your book in all its paperback glory! And it looks amazing.

Honestly, this is the best feeling in the world. Holding your book for the first time. Smelling the pages, flipping through and reading your hard work. It's almost like holding a newborn baby...

But to get here, you must follow a systematic process. It doesn't happen overnight, and there are a few curve balls you'll want to avoid.

This is where Paul's book comes in. As an author, you're already overwhelmed with making sure you're writing is amazing. Now you must worry about formatting, book titles, and cover art? Eek.

It's at this point that a lot of potential best sellers don't make it to market. The thought of publishing a book out into the world is enough to stop even the seasoned of authors dead in their tracks.

I've been there and Paul has too. I've watched Paul grow and excel on his author journey, and in June 2017, he quit his job and go full-time as an author and online educator. He knows how to publish!

He has walked the walk and now can talk the talk, because he's been there, understood how things worked and has had nine successful bestselling books in a short period of time.

I've no doubt that you will learn exactly what you need from this book about publishing; so carefully written and laid out by Paul.

By the end of it, you will be your own little self-publishing rock star, able to hit publish on your book without a care in the world!

I wish you all the success in the world, my little budding author rock star. I encourage you to take notes as you read through Paul's book, but I also want you to take action too. You do not become a bestselling author without following through!

To your success

Lise Cartwright

Indie Author

http://www.hustleandgroove.com

Introduction

Welcome to Book Publishing for Authors. This book will help you with writing, publishing, and launching your book. My goal is to help you through the process of writing your first draft to publishing your book and building your brand. I will also show you additional ways to increase your revenue streams through the sale of paperback books on CreateSpace and audiobooks on Audible.

Chapter 1: The author journey – We start with welcoming you to the journey of an author.

Chapter 2: Advice from bestselling authors – In this chapter I share advice from several Bestselling Authors to assist you in your journey.

Chapter 3: Why are you writing your book – What is the main reason that you are writing your book? Is it to promote a business? Sell personal coaching? Increase public speaking opportunities?

Chapter 4: Idea topics for your book – We will cover idea topics to help you with finding what to write your book about.

Chapter 5: Choosing your book title – In this chapter, we will cover how to choose your book title and show different ways that you can research different book titles to help in your decision.

Chapter 6: Outlining your book – We will cover the outlining process to help you with writing and planning your book.

Chapter 7: Writing your book – In this chapter, we will cover different methods and processes to write (or record via speaking) your book within a span of several weeks. This chapter will help whether you want to have a daily writing schedule or prefer to write when the inspiration hits.

Chapter 8: Editing your book – We will cover how to find an editor as having a great editor is critical in your author journey.

Chapter 9: Formatting your book to Kindle format - MOBI

Chapter 10: Choosing your book cover. (One of the most important parts of having a successful book launch) Having the right cover makes all the difference in a book that will sell and one that will not.

Chapter 11: Creating your book description - otherwise known as, sales copy. Your book description is just as important as having a great book cover design.

Chapter 12: Uploading your book and the process to Amazon and category options for your book.

Chapter 13: How to get book reviews and the challenges involved. It is not an easy process starting out and I will show you methods that I have used to get reviews quickly.

Chapter 14: The free launch strategy - I will cover a launch strategy that can get you thousands of downloads.

Chapter 15: Paid launch strategy at 99 cents. A five-day strategy to help you get sales prior to converting your price from 99 cents to either $2.99 or $3.99.

Chapter 16: How to record an audiobook version of your book - Equipment needed to record it yourself and options to outsource the audiobook recording.

Chapter 17: The process to convert your book into paperback for CreateSpace so that you can also have a paperback edition of your book to sell.

Chapter 18: How to build your audience.

Chapter 19: Lead magnets and why they are critical to building your e-mail list.

Chapter 20: A variety of different back-end products that you can offer your readers.

Chapter 21: Different revenue streams that you can utilize as a Kindle author.

Chapter 22: Summary: The Book Publishing Journey.

I hope that this book helps you in your journey to become a bestselling author. It is a huge commitment to create and market a book. My wish is that this book will help you during your journey. My philosophy in anything I do from teaching, to giving motivational seminars, writing and coaching is to have the power of one. The power of one is my goal to help at least one person and I hope that person is you.

Free Audiobook Offer

Are you a fan of audiobooks? I would like to offer you the audiobook of Motivation 101 for free. All you need to do is go to my website at www.BrodieEDU.com/freeaudiobook and provide your e mail address in exchange for the free digital download. The audiobook will only be available on the website for a limited time as I offer free goodies to my readership on a regular basis.

Chapter 1 The Journey Begins

You have made your decision to take the plunge! It is time to start writing your book. I was in your shoes in June 2015. During that time, I was on a flight to Las Vegas.

I had this book in my head for the previous four years called Eat Less and Move More. The book was about my struggles with weight throughout my life and how I finally got my health together with not only losing over sixty pounds, but also with keeping the weight off.

The problem was that I kept telling myself that I wanted to wait until I reached all my weight goals. I wanted to wait until everything was perfect. Does this sound familiar?

I share a statistic at the start of my Get Published Webinar from the New York Times that showed that 81 percent of Americans feel they have a book in them. How many people have told you that you should write a book?

If you are reading this book or listening to the audiobook, then I bet someone, most likely multiple people have encouraged you to write your own book.

With technology, it is easier than ever to write and publish your own book. All you need is a laptop, word processing software (Microsoft Word or Open Office), an internet connection, and you can channel your author skills into writing the rough draft of your first book within a few days to a few weeks.

After finally getting the inspiration to write my first book, I spent my first morning in Las Vegas outlining Eat Less and Move More on my iPhone. I was inspired to finally get the book ready and to take the plunge. After outlining the book, I then took the literal plunge by jumping in the pool at The Mirage to celebrate. Within one day I had fully outlined my book. I was fired up.

After the Vegas trip, I started writing the book in Microsoft Word in early July. Three days later I had my first manuscript completed and it was over 20,000 words. Now I needed to find an editor.

I met Devin Mooneyham during a motivational seminar I gave in Chicago, IL in 2014. Devin and I stayed in contact and I knew that she offered administrative services. I reached out to her and asked if she edited books. The stars aligned as she immediately said she would love to and is a self-professed, stickler for grammar. I knew that Devin would be perfect to edit my book.

Not only did she edit my first book, but she has edited all my books. Recently we agreed on parameters for Devin to edit my next four books. She is an amazing editor.

Now that I had an editor, I needed a freelancer to format the book to Kindle. In future chapters I will go through this journey and give you people that I personally recommend help you in your own journey to become an author. One thing I want to make crystal clear is that I do not make any money by referring the people who I utilize.

They are recommended because they are all great at what they do and I recommend them because I believe in them. To paraphrase Earnest Hemmingway, it is about the journey and not the destination. The author journey is an amazing adventure.

After my book was edited and formatted I needed to figure out how to market the book. During the rest of July, I spent hundreds of hours learning everything I could about book publishing and how to market my book to bestselling status. It was tough having to learn everything myself.

It ended up working out as I not only was able to publish and market all my books to bestselling status, but now help my clients do the same and all of them have become bestselling authors through my coaching and book publishing system.

Writing and publishing my first book was life changing and in June 2017 I left my job as a Special Education Teacher and am now my own boss, set my own hours, have a ten second commute from my living room to my home office, and can work anywhere in the world with my laptop and internet connection.

One of the main reasons that I wrote this book is to help you speed up the learning curve and put you in position to become a bestselling author soon. Through reading this book, watching my free training, and by joining our Get Published Facebook Community, I am confident that you can accomplish the same thing and become a bestselling author. The journey has officially started.

Chapter 2 Advice from Bestselling Authors

I have been very fortunate with making connections with multiple bestselling authors since starting my own author journey. When I was outlining this book, I wanted to dedicate a chapter to advice from bestselling authors.

I reached out to several of my author pals and asked them a question. The question is very clear and direct and I feel it will help in your author journey.

"Now that you have written and published a bestselling book, what is the one piece of advice that you would give to a first-time author who is currently writing and publishing their book?"

Each author has published at least one bestselling book and the advice they will give in this chapter is outstanding. You will see varied responses from the writing process, publishing process, and marketing strategies.

Let's Begin!

"Being an author is not only about writing. In fact, writing is only 10% of what ends up mattering. I like to abide by Dilbert creator Scott Adam's rule regarding skills: You can't be in the top 1% of writers, you just can't, and you won't be. But being in the top 10% of three different skills will put you far ahead of everyone else. Find the different skills that apply to you."

Patrick King, Multi-time Bestselling Author of books including The Science of Likability, Improve Your People Skills, and Bulletproof Confidence

"Don't be overawed by the size of the task or by your feeling of inadequacy. Simply focus each day on writing something, even if it's only one sentence. So many potential authors start writing, but give up. Fear of what others will think of you, or distractions kill many first-time author's dreams. Discipline yourself to write each day and within several months you'll have the draft of something you'll be very proud of, and something that can help inform, help or entertain many readers. Unleashing the book inside you will be one of your lives greatest achievements. Go for it!"

Barry Watson, Multi-time Bestselling Author of books including Sell With Confidence,

Relationship Rehab, and Rock Solid Relationship

"You have a perspective and writing style that only YOU can offer. Trust yourself in your ability to write something that can impact the lives of your readers."

Dr. Michael Unks, Multi-time Bestselling Author of books including Become the Ace, Awesome in Hours, and The Gym of Life

"I would advise a newbie self-publisher to get that first book published as soon as possible. To illustrate what I mean, my first book, Running A Web Design Business From Home, I wrote in three weeks in a Word document. I uploaded the Word document at KDP and, bam, I was on Amazon. I have since extended the book to about 20,000 words, edited it, and formatted the book to acceptable Kindle and paperback versions. But I got sales on the book and positive reviews. This positive experience showed me how easy publishing was and I've since published another 7 books, most of them bestsellers. You learn by doing. The more books you publish, the better you get at it, the more you sell."

Rob Cubbon, Multi-time Bestselling Author of books including How to Sell Video Courses Online, Free Yourself, and The New Freedom

"Go with your gut. While it's important to seek other people's opinions on content, titles, design and other matters, ultimately this is your project. Don't be afraid to buck the trend and give yourself the final say."

Heidi Farrelly, Multi-time Bestselling Author of books including Mortgage Free and Brilliant Budgets and Despicable Debts

"Before you sit down to write a word or do an outline or pick a title you need to know this – WHO is this book for and WHY should they read it? When you are crystal clear on your answer, then and only then should you put pen to paper (fingertips to keyboard), and keep that person and what your book is giving her in mind the rest of the journey – it will advise your title, your cover design, your angel and your content. The result will be a much tighter book that is easier to read and more beneficial to the reader."

Kylie Ansett, Multi-time Bestselling Author of 10 Years Younger and The Massage Therapist's Success Manual

"The first and foremost question you need to ask yourself is who you are writing this book for and what you want to achieve by publishing it. You need to be honest with yourself because your book's success and your own sense of fulfillment depend on it. If you want to write a book for yourself, or your nearest and dearest – that's OK, go ahead and write it! But if you want to write a book people will want to buy and read, then – think about your audience. Understand your target audience and zero-in on their needs. Do they want to learn, or to be entertained, or maybe both at the same time? Are they looking for inspiration to change their lives, a 'pick-me-up', or an escape from reality? Do they prefer authority or more relaxed tone? Lighthearted or touching stories? Or maybe they don't want to read any stories, just practical advice? Keep your potential readers in mind while working on your book, and that includes the choice of title, subtitle and cover. You can't please everybody ... that's why you should try to please your chosen audience. Because if you really want people to read your book, they need to feel it has been written and published with them in mind."

Joanna Jast, Multi-time Bestselling Author of books including Laser-Sharp Focus and Hack Your Habits

"Dear first-time, author. Don't take yourself too seriously. You may be agonizing over every detail, afraid that you'll get something wrong. I did. Yes, you want your book to be amazing, but avoid searching for perfection. Sometimes art is most powerful when it's raw and unpolished. Want to know a secret? The truth is that making a living as an author is a lot of trial and error. The writing life should be fun, but there's so much pressure to do what everyone else is doing. Advice you will hear: Write faster. Write to market. Launch big. Do it my way. Those things may work for you. They may not. Only you can figure it out over time. Get your first book done. Write at your own pace. Try not to sweat the details so much. There's always your next book."

Courtney Kenney, Multi-time Bestselling Author of books including Creating Space to Thrive, Layoff Reboot, and 100 Awesome Ideas for Authors

"The best advice I can give is the value of being a part of a network of other writers who have the same goal of

becoming a professional writer. The more minds that are thinking alike the better. In these groups, everyone works together toward the same goal of becoming a successful author. Since everyone in the group has their own personalities, experiences, interests, talents, and abilities, the group is a wealth of wisdom. Countless times I have been helped and helped others with titles, sub-titles, formatting, motivation, encouragement, marketing, etc. The key is to participate in the group and help others. If you don't participate and help others, don't expect anyone to help you when you need help. Get involved in the group, participate and be helpful. The more people you help, the better your business will be."

Dustin Heiner, Multi-time Bestselling Author of books including Successfully Unemployed, How to Quit Your Job with Passive Income, and How to Quit Your Job with Rental Properties

"Typing THE END to a novel or a non-fiction book invites an author to stand up, bow, and then break loose in a dance of total elation. After all, we've adhered to our rigid schedule of writing a certain number of words a day for a specific number of days. Right? But typing THE END is only the beginning. Therefore, I have learned to allow three times longer than I thought it

would take to get a book to the finish line. As more and more books are published, the talented and experienced vendors have become busier than ever. Their schedules are out of our control, making it crucial for us to book their services far enough in advance to meet our timelines. Professional cover designers, copy editors, proofreaders, and formatters are often booked three months in advance. It is imperative that we plan accordingly, so we don't have to settle."

Sandra Bass Joines, Multi-time Bestselling Author of books including Spine Surgery Recovery and Tears of Sand

"Find your vibe tribe-the people who believe in the beauty of your dreams. Keep your faith strong by reminding yourself of your purpose, staying positive, and keeping away from cynics."

Cassandra Gaisford, Multi-time Bestselling Author of books including Mid-Life Career Rescue, Find Your Passion and Purpose, and The Art of Success

"Watch out for analysis paralysis, because this could be your brain's sneaky way of letting fear get in the way of finishing your book. It's normal to worry whether or not people will like your work, but don't fall into the trap of researching/planning for so long that you never get around to actually hitting that 'publish' button."

Avery Breyer, Multi-time Bestselling Author of books including Turn Your Computer Into a Money Machine, How to Stop Living Paycheck to Paycheck, and How to Raise Your Credit Score

"My best advice for a new author is going to save time, effort and frustration. This advice is also one of the hardest things I had to make myself do during the writing process. Are you ready for it? Just write and don't edit! It's natural to want to go back and fix spelling and punctuation. I'm saying don't let yourself do any editing until your first draft is done. During the initial writing process, there will be plenty of distractions and editing is one you don't need to add to the mix. That's what editors are for and will all be dealt with after your first draft is finished. When you are writing you want to focus on the writing and nothing else. This will help you finish your book much faster and with a lot less effort. The bottom line is…don't let

anything distract you from the goal of getting your rough draft written."

Dale East, Bestselling Author of Intentional Thinking

"Treat your book like a business. If you want to be a successful author, then you have to look at your book(s) like a business and approach them in the same manner that you would your own job or any other business you're starting. This means setting aside time in your calendar every day to work on your author business. That could be writing your book, working on book title ideas, sharing something on social media or writing blog posts for your website. It means thinking strategically about how you're going to market your book and reach your audience. I know it's not sexy, and you might not think it's fun, but when you treat your books like a business, it takes the emotion out of it (a little, let's be honest, it's like a living, breathing part of us being completely exposed to the world!), allowing you to make decisions based on where you want to take your author business. What are your goals for your book? Who are you trying to reach? The minute I understood this, things shifted for me and I was able to serve my readers better and connect with them more. I also found it a lot easier to make decisions about

marketing my books and what books I'd write next."

Lise Cartwright, Multi-time Bestselling Author of books including Side Hustle Blueprint, Detox Your Diet, and No Gym Needed

"My advice to anyone writing their first book is, find a process and stick with it. Focus on your writing habit in the beginning. I would set a timer for 30 minutes and stay fixed on the writing task during that time. No Internet and downsize your distractions during this focused time. After 30 minutes, take a 5-minute break, then get back into it. Writing a book isn't complicated or difficult; you just have to set yourself up for success. There are several points I will mention here:

1. **Know what you are writing before you show up to write:** *I decide the night before what my writing material will be for the following day. That way, when I show up, I am not just looking at a blank page.*
2. **Write first, edit later:** *I write the first draft in total first. Then, go back and spend 1-2 weeks on a self-edit. Do not edit while you write.*
3. **Sticking with one writing platform.** *Whether you use Microsoft Word, Scrivener or Google Docs, stick with one platform. This will*

eliminate multiple pages of information being gathered in multiple places. Recommend Scrivener for its easy-to-organize features."

Scott Allan, Multi-time Bestselling Author of books including Rejection Reset, Do It Scared, and Relaunch Your Life

"The one piece of advice that I have for a first time Author is to find a mentor. Don't try to re-invent the wheel. Find a mentor that you resonate with and follow in his/her footsteps. And as you do so, make sure that you have fun and enjoy the process!"

Mimi Emmanuel, Multi-time Bestselling Author of books including Live Your Best Life by Writing Your Own Eulogy, My Story of Survival, and God Healed Me

"It won't be perfect. Don't get stuck in overanalyzing each word, each paragraph because it won't be perfect. Writing is a skill that gets ripe with time. As you write more books (if you step on a self-published author career path for a living, you should) your style will refine, you'll find who you want to be in your books, you'll be better and better in your writing and conveying your

message. So don't procrastinate months-or-years – on your first book wishing to make it perfect. Make it decent and publish it. Perfection comes with a learning curve composed of good feedback, bad feedback, experiencing as an author etc. But to get all these, you have to be out there."

Zoe McKey, Multi-time Bestselling Author of books including Budget Like A Pro, Think Different, and Morning Routine Makeover

"The key to being a successful author is completing the process of writing, publishing, and marketing over and repeatedly. You'll get better and better every time. Don't perfect the process. Complete the process. Complete your book. Don't perfect your book. The creative process is messy. Dive in and have some fun."

Tyler Wagner, Multi-time Bestselling Author of books including Conference Crushing, The Better Business Book, and How to Network at Networking Events

Chapter 3 Why Are You Writing Your Book?

One of the biggest questions you need to ask yourself is why are you writing your book? What are you wanting to accomplish? It is critical that you understand the reason for writing your book now.

Writing your first book is a launch pad for many potential projects. Are you wanting to utilize your book to sell a service like public speaking or coaching? Do you want to sell an online course? Are you looking to utilize your book to leave your current job? Is the book going to be to promote your business?

Those are all questions that you need to answer as early as possible. When I have my first call with my clients those are the first questions that I ask. Many of my clients started without a clear vision of where they want to go. After our initial call, I am able to help them get really clear on where they want to go with their book and what they want to accomplish. You must run your book like a business.

This is one of the great benefits of having a book publishing coach or any other coach because they are going to help you with three things. The first is focus. Without having a clear vision on your book, you are not only mudding up the waters regarding your publishing and marketing plan, you are potentially leaving thousands of dollars on the table. The second benefit is accountability. Having a coach is having someone who will keep you accountable for your writing and publishing deadlines and will support you. Benefit number three is implementation.

My philosophy as a book publishing coach is to always give my information freely as you will see throughout this book. A coach makes their living however through the implementation process. Implementation of your writing, publishing and marketing plan is what will make or break your launch at the end of the day.

It is also why I love to work together with my clients either through my Book Publishing for Authors Implementation Program (my favorite option), one-on-one coaching (I only accept a limited number of clients), or through done for you services with publishing your book for you and/or running your book launch for you.

Getting crystal clear on what you want to accomplish with your book as soon as possible will help develop your business plan. One of the toughest things as a coach is when new clients reach out to me and tell me they have already done everything for their book and all they need to do is create a marketing plan. I had one of these calls earlier today as I was writing this chapter. My first question was what was the plan for the back-end? What are they going to offer? Is it public speaking, coaching, online courses? He could not give me a clear answer and was adamant that he must get the book launched within the next month and no more changes could be made after already spending thousands of dollars in publishing costs.

One of the biggest pieces of advice I can give to aspiring authors is to ALWAYS be flexible. It is much easier to do things with flexibility as you will potentially lose out of thousands of dollars by rushing your book. You only get one chance in life to make a first impression. Make sure that you make the best impression possible with your reader because it is a potential life-long relationship.

Chapter 4 Idea Topics for Your Book

Now that you are hopefully clearer on why you are writing your book it is time to figure out what you want to write about. When I started writing my first book, I knew that I wanted it to be about weight loss as many people, including myself struggle with weight. I wanted to write about both the victories and the challenges. I do not feel enough books cover both areas. As an author, you cannot be afraid to be vulnerable in your writing and to share your struggles.

After I wrote Eat Less and Move More I knew that I wanted to start my seminar book series. The first book in the series was called Motivation 101. You can take advantage of the free audiobook offer to listen to Motivation 101 or go to my website and grab the free Kindle version of the book if you prefer to read it.

Motivation 101 is based on one of my motivational seminars. I had two goals with the book. One was to make revenue on the front-end with having the book available in Kindle, Audiobook, and Paperback to maximize revenue streams. When launching your book, you always want to have as many choices as possible because not everyone reads Kindle books. There are some people who love audiobooks and others are old school (like myself) and enjoy reading paperback books.

The other goal was the back-end with promoting the seminar version of Motivation 101. Thanks to the success of the book launch for Motivation 101, I increased my speaking fees where I now charge anywhere from $2500.00 to $5000.00 per seminar.

Through future books in my seminar series I am now able to do the same for Positivity Attracts, The Pursuit of Happiness, Just Do It, and PMA: Positive Mental Attitude. With having the seminar series, it was easy to come up with idea topics for my books.

The same thing happened with my travel series. I love to travel, especially to Maui and Las Vegas. It was suggested many times in the past that I should write a travel book because of all the research I do in planning trips and how it could help a lot of people with their vacation. I wrote Maui in summer 2016 while staying there and it opened several benefits including tax benefits, bringing in new clients who wanted to write their own travel books, and getting to help people with their future trips.

Since that trip, I have written and published another travel bestseller about San Diego and will be writing a second book about Maui when I am there once again in mid-October 2017 when this book is released. Future books are planned about Las Vegas and potentially Miami.

My main advice is to find what you love writing about. Whether that is about travel, creating seminar versions of your books, children's books, or fiction books, find something that you will enjoy writing about. The more that you enjoy the idea topic, the easier it will be to write a book about the subject.

If you are writing a book about your business, whether that is to promote a travel agency, construction business, medical products or programs, make sure it is something that you feel strongly about. Readers can tell if you are serious about a subject and will connect with you, especially if you are helping them solve a problem.

I recently was able to get my dad to agree to write a book. He is one of the most successful business people I have ever known. My dad has the equivalent of a tenth-grade education and he has always worried that if he wrote a book on his business, it would be unsuccessful due to his perceived lack of education.

What I explained to my dad is that writing a book is just like giving a motivational seminar. It is having a louder conversation with a friend. Once I could make that connection with him, he realized that he didn't even have to write a book.

Instead, we are going to record the book via conversations between my dad and myself. I am planning to send the recordings to a freelancer to have them transcribe the conversations. At that point, we will work together to clean up the book and have it edited. Once that is done, I will record the audiobook version as that also serves as a great way to do one final proofread of your book and set up the book launch. The book is about his business where he sells walk-in refrigerator panels and how he has built his company significantly over the past several years.

In the book, he is going to cover his journey in sales and business and is going to educate the reader on how to utilize walk-in panels to build items ranging from food trucks, tiny houses, and mobile homes. The book will be used to promote his company and generate leads.

I share this story because I believe that anyone can write and publish a book. As a teacher, I learned that everyone learns differently through various learning styles. The same goes for different ways of communication. If you are not comfortable with writing a book, then you can create a book through recorded conversations or even content from webinars.

My business coach, Taki Moore, did this with his book. It is called Million Dollar Coach and is the best book I have read this year. He wrote the book through his communication style of webinars and a little writing, and did an amazing job with connecting with the reader. What is even more amazing is that he actually recorded the webinars and put them together with the book in five hours. That's right, he created his book in five hours.

There are many idea topics from which to choose. They can be to promote your business, encourage travel to great destinations, promote motivational, leadership, or educational seminars, help people with their battles with weight, or about book publishing, like this book.

I also encourage you to search for books on Amazon. Through these methods, I am confident that you will find great ideas for topics.

Chapter 5 Choosing Your Book Title

Have you decided on your book title? When it comes to choosing a book title you want to choose a title that will be easy to search for on Amazon.

Amazon is essentially a giant search engine. When you type in certain phrases you will notice this trend. I suggest trying this yourself. Once you are on Amazon go to the search engine on Amazon, go to the search tab on the left side of the search bar, change search tab from "all departments" to "kindle store".

If you already have chosen your book title, then type in the first word of the book title and see what comes up in the search results. Your book title does need to connect with the content in your book.

Some great book title examples are: The 4 Hour Workweek, Awaken The Giant Within, How to Win Friends and Influence People, To Kill a Mockingbird, Rich Dad Poor Dad, The 7 Habits of Highly Effective People.

What makes those titles great? The titles are eye-catching and get your attention. The titles are also easy to understand. When I decided on Eat Less and Move More for my first book, I wanted the title to connect with fitness, my own journey, and the point of the book, the outcome.

As a teacher for nine years, one of the greatest lessons I have learned is that we must make things as simple as possible. Don't make an overly complex or complicated title. You also want to have a strong subtitle.

The subtitle of your book is the benefit to the reader. For example, most of my books focus on ten ways to help the reader. In Motivation 101 the subtitle is Ten Ways to Increase Your Motivation. The subtitle is clear with the benefit to the reader with Ten Ways to Increase Your Motivation. Remember the subtitle always should be about the benefit to your reader.

When I created my third book I already decided on the title as it was based on one of my motivational seminars. The book was called Positivity Attracts. If you type the word positivity in Amazon, the results are quite impressive. Anything with the work positive or a variation of the word (like positivity) gets many search results on Amazon.

The subtitle of Positivity Attracts showed the benefit with Ten Ways to Improve Your Positive

Thinking. My subtitles are typically short and to the point. Simplicity is always best with choosing both your title and subtitle.

Chapter 6 Outlining Your Book

Outlining the book will help you plan the content of your book. My first experience outlining a book was at the pool at The Mirage Casino in Las Vegas. During that morning, I spent around an hour coming up with the outline while enjoying the morning summer heat in Sin City.

When creating your first draft do not worry about it being perfect. The main thing is to create a game plan through writing out your outline. Writing out the outline will help get you clear on what you want to write in your book. It will also help you with the pace and timeline of your writing content.

Another nice benefit is once you outline your book you will see potential opportunities to expand your book into book series. When I wrote Motivation 101, Chapter 4 of the book was called Just Do It. I found a lot of great content with that chapter where I could create another book that was released during Thanksgiving 2016.

It was called Just Do It and began as a chapter in Motivation 101, then became a seminar and then eventually evolved into my seventh bestselling book. When I originally created my first seminar in 2007 it was called PMA: Positive Mental Attitude. It was a motivational seminar that later became my eighth bestselling book. Through that seminar, I always created new content. The additional content from PMA became Positivity Attracts. Once I had enough new content for Positivity Attracts the next seminar created was Motivation 101. When I had enough content for Motivation 101 I created the seminar for The Pursuit of Happiness.

After I had enough content for The Pursuit of Happiness the next seminar became Just Do It. When I had everything completed and updated for Just Do It, I created Be Your Greatest Champion.

I share this process because of the power of outlining your content. All my original seminars had outlines and it was easy to translate the outlines to the books. You can do the same thing with your content, otherwise known as IP. Your IP is your Intellectual Property. The IP is your content that you create for your books, seminars, online coaching, courses etc. It is the knowledge that you have which you turned into your content.

Outlining is a great way to be clear on what you are going to write. The best part is that you will most likely be able to find more content then you need for your book. You can utilize the additional content to create additional books as part of a book series.

Having an outline provides you with clarity as you write your book. The outline will also help ensure that your book flows and connects with the title, subtitle, and content throughout your book.

Chapter 7 Writing Your Book

Now that you have your book title, subtitle, and outline, it is time to start writing your book. You can accomplish this two ways.

When writing your book, you can write it in the order of your outline or you can write it out of the outline order. Typically, I recommend writing your book in the order of your outline. However, if there is a chapter that you absolutely must write first then I encourage you to do so.

One of the main questions that I get from my clients is how much time should I set aside each day to write? Everyone is different with his or her writing process. There is not a universal process for everyone.

What I typically like to find out is my client's process. Are they the type of person who highly organizes their day? If that is the case, I recommend they block out one – two hours a day to write their book. The potential goal could be to write a chapter a day.

If my clients are more like me and prone to writing when the inspiration hits, then I recommend starting to write as much as you can in one sitting. I always recommend taking brakes every ninety minutes to get a drink, take a break, and get up and stretch.

Everyone is going to be different and you need to find the style that fits you best. For my own books, I have written several of the books over three to four days. When I wrote Positivity Attracts, I literally could not stop writing and in one day had written over ten thousand words for the book. Again, it depends on your own personal writing style.

Using either method will ensure that you have your book completed within two - three weeks. I recommend that you have someone who will keep you accountable with your book writing. Whether that is investing in a book publishing coach like myself, or relying on a good friend or family member, having accountability, focus, and encouragement throughout the writing process is critical.

If you have my style of writing and write when the inspiration hits, then give yourself a goal to write your books in three weeks. That way you have a deadline and know that even though you are not specifically setting time to write your book each day, that you do need to have your book done in three weeks. You could also set the goal to write four chapters in a week to get started. Again, you must figure out what is the best route for you. Deadlines will make all the difference in getting your book written.

Regardless of which method you use, realize that your book doesn't have to be perfect. Once the book is written, do not second-guess yourself. You have already taken the plunge and now it is time to send off your first draft to your editor.

Before we more on, I want to share the feedback that I received from one of my students that is currently in the Book Publishing for Authors Implementation program. I am sharing her feedback in this chapter as Elizabeth's goal has been to write a book for the past forty years.

"Joining Paul Brodie's 'Book Publishing for Authors Implementation Program' has re-ignited my passion for writing. Mr. Brodie's coaching expertise, encouragement, inspiration and transparency has motivated me to pursue my forty-year dream of composing non-fiction books. Through his extremely user friendly and in-depth weekly Training Modules, he leaves no stone unturned as he shares his personal experiences about manuscripts, book covers and titles, editors, publishers, etc. Mr. Brodie also provides invaluable real-time on-line Live Group Coaching.

During these sessions, he not only answers my questions on the spot, he communicates through email after the Webinar is over. I highly recommend Mr. Brodie's program to anyone seeking the same dream I have of becoming a published author. I am going on sixty years of age and experiencing the reality of it is never too late to put that pen to paper and let your words flow. Cheers to you, Paul Brodie!" Elizabeth Vidad

At this point, we have completed the writing process and will next move to the publishing part of the book. I do want you to think about the following question.

Please write down what has been the most useful to you so far before you move on to the publishing part of the book.

Chapter 8 Editing Your Book

Having a great editor is critical to the success of your book. An editor will typically catch eighty to ninety percent of your mistakes and will not only find the mistakes, but will also make suggestions or corrections.

A poorly edited book with multiple spelling mistakes will cost you both short-term and long-term sales through refunds from unhappy readers. You could get negative reviews due to multiple spelling, grammar, and punctuation mistakes. An editor will find most, if not all your errors. Remember that a poorly edited book will hurt not only your books, but also your brand and business.

An editor could be a friend or family member or you can find a freelancer on Fiverr or Upwork. You can also ask other authors who they would recommend. The most important thing is to find a quality editor for your book as you only get one chance to make a first impression with your readers.

In July 2015, I wrote my first book Eat Less and Move More over three days. After my first draft was ready to go, I reached out to a friend of mine who is an excellent book editor. Her name is Devin Mooneyham and she has served as the editor for all my books. Devin sliced and diced my first draft editing the grammatical errors, sentence fragments, and took out parts of chapters that did not flow.

I trusted Devin completely with this huge part of the process and ever since our partnership has been wonderful. Having a great editor is critical and something I consider the most crucial part of finishing your book.

You can find very good editors on Fiverr.com or on Upwork.com or you can reach out to Devin at Mooneyham.Devin@gmail.com. Editing can range anywhere from one hundred dollars to five hundred dollars, so finding the right editor is very important. The fee will also vary depending on how many words are in your book. If your book is over twenty-five thousand words, then you can expect to pay more for an editor as the editing process can be very time consuming.

After you have gone through your first, second, and final draft with your editor, I highly recommend one final process that I have already touched on briefly. This is also going to connect with the audiobook chapter that we will cover later in this book.

When you record the audiobook version of your book it also serves as one final opportunity to proofread your book. This tends to be the best way to read a final proof. For my books, I have at least three people read it to catch errors, but no matter what, you will always find errors. That's part of being human. I found errors in all my books while proofreading. Most of the errors found while proofreading is between five to ten small spelling or grammatical errors per book. It's going to happen and the best way to catch those final errors is to read the book aloud yourself.

You also need to decide whether you want to record the audiobook for your first book. I chose not to and did a royalty share agreement on Audible. The royalty share agreement is when you hire someone else to narrate your book. Audible has many different narrators and they will audition for you. That way you can choose the voice that you prefer. Typically, the royalty for making your audiobook exclusive to Audible is forty percent. If your book is non-exclusive to Audible your royalty drops to twenty-five percent, but you can sell the audiobook yourself or give it away to build your email list.

When you enter a royalty share agreement with a narrator, you split the forty percent exclusive royalty with them. You will get twenty percent and your narrator gets twenty percent. You will also split evenly any bounties that you receive. I will go into bounties in more detail later in this book. Twenty percent of something is better than forty percent of nothing.

If you end up doing a royalty share agreement and have a narrator record the audiobook for you then I still recommend reading the book aloud for one final proofread. You will be amazed how many small errors you find. Even with having multiple people proofread your book after having been edited, no book will be perfect.

I had a client who had two editors and still found errors after giving it one final proofread. Proofreading it one final time is an easy process. If you are just going to read it out loud I would suggest either reading it out loud to yourself or read it to a family member or friend.

You do not have to read out the entire book in one sitting. I would recommend reading one chapter in the morning and another chapter in the evening. If you do this for a few days then you will have everything read aloud within a week.

You can also read all the front matter in one morning session and then read all the back matter in the evening out loud. The front matter will be your disclaimer, dedication, back-end offer with speaking, coaching, or online course, and usually a gift like an audiobook version of your book or a chapter of an upcoming book to give away in exchange for the reader's email address to join your list. We will cover the front and back matter later in the book.

The best part of reading it out one chapter at a time is that you can correct any minor errors very quickly. The errors that you find in the proof will be minor with a misspelled word, or grammar error showing up possibly one or two times in a chapter.

Once you have written your second book I do recommend recording the audiobook yourself and I will go more into detail about that process in our audiobook chapter. I did want to share with you some of the information about audiobooks in this chapter as it connects with the editing process. In my view, there is no better way to proofread your book then recording the audiobook version yourself.

When you find the right editor, I recommend building a long-term relationship with them. The more you work with the same person, the better the editing becomes as they get to know your writing style. Devin has done an incredible job with not only the edits, but also with keeping my tone and message.

Once the editing process is completed, it is then time to move on to getting your book formatted to Kindle.

Chapter 9 Formatting Your Book to Kindle

Once your final draft is complete, edited, and proofread then you will need to convert your book to MOBI format for Kindle. Fiverr and Upwork have many freelancers who will convert your word file to MOBI. It will typically cost between twenty-five and fifty dollars for the conversion. You can also do it yourself with a program called Scrivener.

I have Scrivener, but do not use it because I prefer my final draft converted to Kindle through outsourcing as many things can go wrong with MOBI conversions. Scrivener does have a learning curve, but other author friends of mine love it once they get used to it. My preference is to write my books in Microsoft Word as that is the process that I am comfortable with. When you are writing your book, you want the process to be as comfortable as possible.

I feel comfortable using word and have done so for all my books. The freelancer I use is gigsterready on Fiverr (www.fiverr.com/gigsterready) and she typically takes three to four days to complete the conversion, but she does great work. Eat Less and Move More after edits and proofreading was over eighteen thousand words and cost fifty dollars to convert. Both Motivation 101 and Positivity Attracts were thirty dollars each for the conversion as both books were a little over nine thousand words after edits and proofreading.

If your book has multiple pictures then the conversion does cost a little more. My travel books have many pictures so those conversions do cost me between fifty and sixty-five dollars as the pictures must be compressed for the Kindle version.

Formatting to Kindle is a process that I prefer to outsource to a freelancer. I would recommend that you outsource at least your first book to a freelancer. If you want to use Scrivener or another program to format your book, then do what you feel is best for you. With my clients, I always want to make the writing and publishing of your first book as easy as possible as there are many moving parts in a book launch, especially when it is the launch of your first book.

Chapter 10 Choosing Your Book Cover

Having a great looking book cover is one of the most important parts about having a successful book launch. Readers do judge a book by its cover and you will want to have the best-looking book cover possible.

When you are deciding on your book cover, you want to look at several factors. You want the cover to be eye-catching. It needs to grab the attention of the reader.

You also want to have great colors in the cover. Orange has proven to sell well as that color not only stands out, but also elicits a buying response in potential customers. Having a bold font in the book title is also important, as you want to have the actual title stand out.

As I mentioned previously, the subtitle is also crucial and tells readers the benefits of your book. You want to have a very clear subtitle and tell the reader why your book will help them solve a problem.

The cover also needs to look great in the thumbnail view on Amazon. When you do a search of books on Amazon you will see the results in list form. The book covers will be in a much smaller format, otherwise known as a thumbnail view. Having a great looking cover with a clear and bold title will stand out, especially when competing with other books for the reader's attention.

The thumbnail view also comes into play on book sales rankings. When you click on a book you will see the books ranking and will be able to click on that ranking and see other books in that category. Your book cover is shown in the thumbnail form and again will stand out if it looks good.

The book cover is your window dressing. Choosing the right book cover is critical to your book becoming a successful, potential #1 bestseller, or just another book. Covers can range in cost from several dollars to hundreds of dollars. As I had a small budget for my first book, Eat Less and Move More, I knew that I needed to get as much bang for the buck as possible.

I researched Fiverr extensively and found a freelancer who made book covers for a very inexpensive cost and had a great rating from customers. In fact, she has thousands of ratings so I figured I would give it a shot. I was not disappointed.

Everything on Fiverr is at least five dollars to start, but there are always extras. I chose the twenty-dollar option for my first three books, which included the five-dollar gig, an additional five dollars for a high-quality stock image, and ten dollars for the original PSD file and PDF. This was a great investment so I could have the master copy in case I ever needed to make any changes.

In my request for my first book cover, I asked for a blue and black color scheme. Within four days, my designer delivered my first book cover and I loved it.

I knew similarly to Devin, that I found a potential long-term partner for my books. Vikiana has made all my book covers and she has done an incredible job for an amazing low price. This was the book cover design that Vikiana created for my first book.

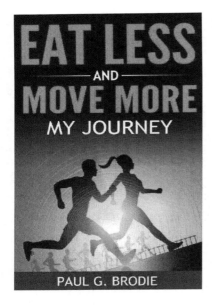

It is one of my favorite covers. As you can see, my subtitle was not strong. In 2018, I am writing and publishing the sequel for Eat Less and Move More and have a subtitle with a definable outcome like my other books. In the sequel, I have the subtitle as Ten Ways to Help You Lose Weight and Keep the Weight Off. With that book, I have a clear subtitle with a definable outcome.

If I ever go back and change the first book, I will add more of a definable outcome. I was still proud of the title and subtitle overall and how the book started to build the momentum in my own journey as my first bestselling book.

I had a different problem with Motivation 101, my second book. Problem was that I hated the book cover. Here is the original cover.

The cover did not fit. Seeing the ugly brown shoes in additional to the poor placement of the subtitle made me realize that my second book would not be successful if I launched the book with that cover. I decided that I needed to make a change.

I reached out Vikiana and created a new order. In the order, I told her that I wanted a new cover and my vision for the cover was of a sunset with Motivation 101 still in bold on top of the cover. I also made clear that I wanted the subtitle just below the main title. This is what she created for me for five dollars (six dollars with service fee) as I did not order any extras since it was a new design.

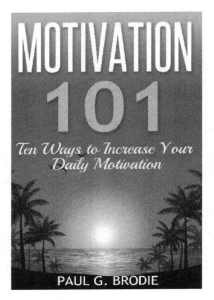

The cover was a huge upgrade and I felt great about the book cover. I ordered additional covers for the audiobook version and the paperback version. Typically, you can order the audiobook cover version for ten dollars and the paperback version will cost you twenty-five dollars. I knew that the new cover would help make my second book a bestseller and it did.

Before we wrap up this chapter, I want to share with you how you can design your own cover. I am a terrible artist and cannot draw at all. However, I can do some basic design concepts. If I can create a rough mockup of a cover then anyone can.

When I think of a book cover design, I do searches on google. I find images that I feel will fit the cover and then figure out the placement of where I want the title, subtitle, background cover, and image design. You always want your title on the top part of your book.

When creating a book cover you want to be able to see the book cover in both a regular and thumbnail view. Once you have a general idea of what you want then you can send the information to your book designer and make clear what you want in the cover design.

One thing I will do is create a mock design in Microsoft Word. I will create the book title with the font and color that I want. Below will be the design that I want in the cover. Once everything is done, I will send it to my cover designer. Currently I pay for the basic gig with Fiverr at the five-dollar price and will pay an additional five dollars to have Vikiana use a stock image in the design. With the one dollar service fee, I end up paying eleven dollars for the Kindle version of the book cover, eleven dollars (ten dollars plus the one dollar service fee) for the audiobook cover, and twenty-five dollars (twenty-six dollars with the service fee) for the paperback cover.

One thing I would recommend is making things very clear to Vikiana about your paperback cover if you end up using her service. Make sure you tell her both your book size and the number of pages that are in your book. The only problem I have had with her designs is the occasional issue with her paperback covers so make sure you are clear with your book specifications. Her Kindle and audiobook covers are excellent. Whether you go with Vikiana or another designer on Fiverr, make sure you find a book cover designer that has a lot of reviews and a high rating. You can find several great designers on Fiverr and Upwork.

By using that process, you should be able to come up with a great book cover design. I also recommend downloading book covers that you like on Amazon that you feel stand out. Create a folder on your computer with the title, book covers, and save every book cover that you like in that file. You will have a great library of book covers to help you find inspiration for your book cover design.

If you are looking for some great book cover designs then check out my own book page at www.BrodieEDU.com/books to get some ideas. I also recommend looking up the following book covers: The 4 Hour Workweek, The Devil Wears Prada, To Kill A Mockingbird, Rich Dad Poor Dad, The 7 Habits Of Highly Effective People.

Chapter 11 Creating Your Book Description

The book description is also known as your sales copy. This is what will help sell your book. The goal of your book description should be to help the reader identify a problem that you will help solve. There is a great article from New York Times Bestselling Author, Kevin Kruse, which explains how to write sales copy that I highly recommend - you can check it out here. I came upon this resource while my third book, Positivity Attracts was getting ready to launch.

For my first book, Eat Less and Move More, I researched many top authors and looked at their styles. After looking at many book descriptions, I came up with the following for Eat Less and Move More.

Eat Less and Move More: My Journey shows you how you can **change your lifestyle** *without spending long hours in the gym and without starving yourself while enjoying cheat meals.*

On May 2, 2011, I received my wake-up call. I was 336 pounds, had borderline type 2 diabetes, and was recently recovered from both bronchitis and pneumonia. My bad eating habits and lifestyle choices were making me ill, but I was too wrapped up in what I was doing to spot the signs let alone to do anything about it. **That day I found myself in the doctor's office and was told that I might not be around in 5-10 years if I didn't change my**

lifestyle. That was my wake-up call. Luckily I got a second chance.

That day I realized that <u>life is short and precious</u> and I made a decision that I was going to do things differently. I decided to change my life so that I could **live life to the fullest** and **eat less and move more**.

What I decided to create for myself was:

- A healthy lifestyle that **I could be proud of**
- The **mental freedom** to live the life of my dreams
- The **freedom of good health** to do the things I love and to be with the people who matter most to me

And now I want to help you do the same.

After all, deciding to start your journey to **eat less and move more** is something you do because you have a vision of a better life for you and your family. **It's your chance to take control and live life on your terms**. And done right *<u>it will give you</u> the mental freedom and the freedom of good health to do the things you love, when you want to do them and <u>with</u> the people who matter most in your life.*

Eat Less and Move More will show you how to create an improved you that gives you the time to work on your own passions in life. It will also show you the mistakes that I made and what I did when I gained over half of the weight back. I also tell my story throughout the book of working in the corporate world and eventually leaving that world to pursue a career in teaching as my weight and career were connected.

In short, losing weight and keeping the weight off is not a

temporary change but a lifestyle choice by choosing to **eat less and move more.**

Eat Less and Move More shows you how you can easily start your own **journey towards a healthier lifestyle** – a lifestyle that you can be proud of <u>and</u> achieve both **mental freedom** and **freedom of good health.**

But more than this, Eat Less and Move More explores what it means to live a truly happy and fulfilled life – to *really live the life of your dreams and pursue what you love.* It encourages you to examine your own motivations and desires in order to **determine your path in life.**

To get access to the bonus materials and resources (all for FREE), be sure to visit:

www.BrodieEDU.com

It was not bad for my first launch, but after reading Kevin's article, I changed my approach for sales copy and created the following sales copy for Eat Less and Move More. I made these changes in late November 2015. One of the best things about Kindle is that you can change and update your book and change your book description whenever you want to.

Here is the new and improved sales copy.

Eat Less and Move More: My Journey shows how you can **change your mindset** and **improve your physical and mental health**.

What if a few new habits could improve your personal health? What if you could increase your health and happiness with a few simple steps? Imagine waking up in the morning feeling healthy and happy and ready to take on the day.

Amazon bestselling author, Paul G. Brodie, in his first book, covers multiple ways to improve your physical and mental health.

Here are a few things that you will get out of Eat Less and Move More.

In this book, you will learn.

- How to learn to Listen to Your Body
- How to take a Leap of Faith and Follow Your Dreams
- How to respond when your body gives you a Wakeup Call
- How to Eat Less and Move More
- How to respond if you gain weight after an initial weight loss
- How to create a healthy environment by Eating Clean
- How to Change Your Lifestyle at any age

- How to utilize Healthy Eating Habits in your everyday life
- How to enjoy Cheat Meals without feeling guilty
- BONUS: Daily Food Lists for what Paul has utilized to lose over sixty pounds and current food items that he eats to continue to live a healthy lifestyle

Buy this book NOW to increase your personal, physical and mental health

Pick up your copy today by clicking the BUY NOW button at the top of this page!

As you can see, I made a much better effort in identifying a problem for the reader and offering solutions. In addition, I added two calls to action at the end of the sales copy by telling the reader to buy now. Calls to action may sound basic, but they do work.

When you write your book description, remember that the first sentence that you write is the big promise. This is what the reader will get out of your book. With Eat Less and Move More the first sentence was change your mindset and improve your physical and mental health.

Once you have written your first sentence with the big promise, you will want to follow with two additional benefits of buying your book. Using "what if" and "imagine" statements are great ways to start the two additional benefits.

The book description needs to describe the content of your book with benefits to the reader. Another thing you can do is offer bonuses in the description. In my Maui book, I offer a free travel guide as one of the bonuses.

As you approach the end of your book description, you want to restate the big promise again. With Eat Less and Move More I added buy this book NOW to increase your personal physical and mental health.

At the end of the book description, you want to close them with BUY NOW. Here is how I close Eat Less and Move More, pick up your copy today by clicking the BUY NOW button at the top of this page.

Once you have completed your sales copy you will need to have it converted to html. I found a freelancer on Fiverr called Kindleserge who converted my sales copy for five dollars. Once you get the file back, it will be in a txt file. I have utilized Kindleserge for my first three launches. I have learned more about html since then and created the html update myself for the book descriptions since early 2016.

At this point, you will want to go to Amazon and to Author Central. In Author Central, you can add your personal information with an author bio and pictures. When you are ready to upload your book, you will have the option to add your sales copy in the book description. With the html code, the sales copy will stand out and you will have the ability to bold words to help grab the reader's attention. The book description should also be used in the back of your paperback book, which we will cover later.

Chapter 12 Uploading Your Book and Kindle Direct Publishing

I strongly recommend uploading your book one week prior to your official launch. To upload your book to Amazon you will need the MOBI file, the book cover, and your book description. The instructions are simple to follow on Amazon for this process if you have those three files.

You will need to set up a KDP Amazon account first at https://kdp.amazon.com. Follow the instructions, as it is an easy process. Once your account is set up then sign in and go to bookshelf. Go to create a new title, select Kindle eBook and click on the plus icon. You will have three pages to fill out. Those pages are Kindle eBook details, Kindle eBook content, and Kindle eBook pricing.

When you are uploading your book, you will have the option to sign up for Kindle Direct Publishing (KDP) Select. Taking advantage of this will help with your launch and it allows you to choose one of two promotions. The only drawback is that your eBook will be exclusive to Amazon for 90 days. You can then take your eBook out of KDP after the 90-day period if you choose to.

In KDP Select, either you can choose five free days for your promo (which I suggest) or you can have a Kindle countdown where you can sell your book for 99 cents for seven days and still get your 70 percent royalty. The only drawback with Kindle countdown is that your book must be on Amazon for thirty days before you can utilize the Kindle countdown. Usually, when your book is under $2.99 your book will only be eligible for a 35 percent royalty. With the Kindle countdown, you get 70 cents instead of 35 cents at the 99-cent price point.

I suggest choosing the five-day free promo, but we will get to that later in the book. The goal as a new author is to get your book into as many hands as possible. The best way to do that is to utilize the free promotion so you have the potential to get your books to thousands of readers and those readers can purchase your future books, sign up for your e-mail list, and purchase back-end products including coaching, courses, etc.

By signing up in KDP select, you will also be enrolled in the KDP Select Global Fund. The fund is for both Kindle Unlimited and the Kindle Owners Lending Library. You are paid for each page a potential customer reads of your book.

The Kindle Unlimited program is essentially Netflix for Amazon Kindle where for a flat fee; the reader gets unlimited Kindle books to read. You do get a percentage of revenue based on how many pages (called Kindle Edition Normalized Pages/KNEP) are read. It is not a huge amount, but over time, with a lot of pages read, it can add up. You do have the option to sign up for the Kindle Owners Lending Library where readers that buy your book can lend the Kindle book to a friend or family member. Again, the goal is to get as many people to read your eBook as possible so I recommend signing up for the Kindle book lending option.

Another great resource is the Kindle MatchBook. The Kindle MatchBook option gives readers who bought the paperback edition of your book the option to either purchase the Kindle version for $1.99, 99 cents or free. I go with the 99 cents option since the reader has already bought your paperback edition, they will most likely take advantage of the discount and it will count as a sale. You will get 52 cents per sale at the 99-cent price point through Kindle MatchBook.

Next comes choosing your sales categories. You are responsible for selecting two categories for your book. It is CRUCIAL to have your book in two different categories if you want to be as successful as possible. Furthermore, where you place your book is extremely critical too. For my books, I looked at two main categories with Business & Money and Biographies & Memoirs. Both main categories are ones that sell very well. I also wanted to get into as many sub categories in those areas as possible.

For example, in Motivation 101 I placed the book into the following category. Kindle Store>Kindle eBooks>Business & Money>Economics>Urban & Regional. I chose the main category as Business & Money, then dug deeper to find deeper categories inside Business & Money. In Urban & Regional I found a deep category to place my book that was not highly competitive. Motivation 101 was #1 in that category during the launch and for several months afterwards. Your book also will show up in multiple categories with finding a deeper category. For example, Motivation 101 was #1 in Urban & Regional and in the top books in Economics and in Business & Money. Your book and rating are shown in many categories, which help to increase traffic to your book. This is especially beneficial during your launch, as your book will be showing up in the hot new releases section of all those categories for the first month.

I typically choose a category that is not highly competitive for the first category and then find a tougher category for the second. For overall ranking, look for the top three books in the categories ranked from 5000-10000 overall in Amazon Kindle. Those are great categories to place your books. With Motivation 101 I put the book in the following second category Kindle Store>Kindle eBooks>Nonfiction>Self-Help>Creativity. There are many categories to look at and it is important to find a category that has the top ranked books ranked around 10,000 to 20,000 in Amazon Kindle. Having your book as the top ranked book in your category also gives you that great orange sticker from Amazon that says Amazon #1 bestseller in that category. Potential readers are typically impressed when a book shows that it is a bestseller.

Once you upload your book, you will need to set a price. As I mentioned, I set my price at 99 cents. The drawback is that it is only a 35 percent royalty versus 70 percent for $2.99. However, each unit on Amazon counts as a unit sold regardless of the price. Having the price at 99 cents will help boost early sales and with getting reviews prior to the official book launch.

Chapter 13 Getting Reviews

Getting reviews is one of the toughest things to do as an author. For your first launch, I would suggest reaching out to friends, family, acquaintances, and Facebook friends to get honest reviews. Your goal by the first week of uploading your book to Amazon is to get at least five to ten reviews.

To build your momentum for your book launch you want to have at least ten to fifteen reviews by the end of your launch. Book reviews help Amazon potentially promote your book as a hot new release. Having a lot of book reviews shows social proof that your book is worth buying.

Book reviews are challenging to get. You need to have multiple strategies to reach out to reviewers and you cannot be timid with asking for reviews.

I ended up contacting over 100 people for my first book launch. Out of those 100-people contacted, only 12 people submitted reviews. The good part is that once you get to know fellow authors in Facebook groups then you are eventually able to build upon your brand and you will get more reviews. This has proven as Eat Less and Move more had 17 reviews, Motivation 101 had 22 reviews and Positivity Attracts after only a few weeks on Amazon has 33 reviews by the end of the launch phase.

For your first book through the process will be tough. People you think you can rely on will most likely let you down. One of the things I would recommend is to do the strategy that I did for my third book, Positivity Attracts.

One strategy I found to be helpful was uploading the final version of the PDF file to Dropbox and then sending the link to fellow author pals and a few friends that are always helpful and leave reviews for me on both Amazon and Goodreads. You will want reviews on both pages as Goodreads readers can be very critical about books. They are very passionate and tend to consider very good books to be only 3 to 4 stars while Amazon readers will typically grade your book as 4 to 5 stars.

Be sure to send follow up messages to your potential reviewers too. I would recommend sending out the advance copies a week before you upload your book to Amazon. Once you upload to Amazon, send a follow up message to ask if they had a chance to read the book. Let them know that the book is uploaded and is available for 99 cents and that you could really use their support by downloading a copy and leaving you a review.

I have found this to work well, but I would not recommend contacting the same person more than four times.

Another tactic that you can do is creating a book launch group on Facebook. You can invite your Facebook friends to the group and post regularly in the group. I had a Facebook group for my third launch. I would say that I received fifteen reviews in my launch group for Positivity Attracts, which was helpful.

Another way to add social proof to your book launch is utilizing editorial reviews. You will use parts of reviews from people who leave you reviews. Editorial reviews will show up on your book page before all other reviews.

You can create editorial reviews by setting up your Amazon author central page at https://authorcentral.amazon.com. Do not set up the page until after your book is live on Amazon. It is an easy process to follow. I am going to show you examples of editorial reviews from my PMA: Positive Mental Attitude book.

Editorial Reviews

"Paul Brodie does it, yet again. This is another classic sure to give you insight and actionable tips."
- **Shawn Richardson, Author**

"If you do nothing but read this book and take the time to ask the questions the author poses then honestly answer them, you will gain far more than the price you paid for admission."
- **Dale East, Amazon Bestselling Author of Intentional Thinking**

"What I love about Paul's writing is the fact he gets straight to the heart of what his content is trying to get across. No superfluous stories to bulk up the page count, just wisdom."
- **Ayodeji Awosika, Author and Personal Development Blogger**

"In a climate that is need of positivity, the book helps to keep your mind positive. It is a must read!"
- **Amazon Customer**

"PMA is a fantastic little book chock-full of inspiring wisdom and great stories to support the topic."

- Scott Allan, Amazon Bestselling Author of Do It Scared

"Read the Chapter on Priorities. Few people know how to prioritize. This chapter brought tears to my eyes. This author knows how to prioritize. We can all learn a lesson from him."
- Amazon Customer

"The book will have you feeling healthy, happy and terrific!"
- Amazon Customer

"Very direct and to the point. Packs valuable information in a short read. Each chapter has specific exercises and journaling questions to really integrate the value of what is being shared."
- Amazon Customer

Having editorial reviews will help with adding social proof to your book page. Getting reviews is a tedious and time-consuming process. You want to reach out to as many people as possible, especially for your first book launch. Remember that your goal is to have at least ten to fifteen reviews by the end of your book launch.

You can do it! Persistence is key to a successful book launch.

Chapter 14 Free Launch Strategy

During the launch process, there are two parts to the marketing side of launching your book. The first part is the free launch strategy that we will cover in this chapter.

The free launch strategy will help get your book into the hands of as many people as possible. What I first suggest is to decide whether you want to do a four or five-day strategy for your free launch. Again, as an author who is starting out I would suggest going the free route to get your book into as many hands as possible.

After deciding whether you want to go the four or five-day route, you will want to decide on dates. My launches always start on Sunday. On Sunday morning, I create a status update on Facebook about my book being free to encourage people to check it out while free. I also post it on Twitter and Instagram.

Here is an example of what I recommend doing on a free launch.

Sunday Day #1. BKnights Promotion (costs $5.00 on Fiverr.com)

Monday Day #2. Freebooksy Promotion (costs $80.00 on freebooksy.com). This is the best investment that you can make in my view for your free launch. This day your book is most likely to rank highest.

Tuesday Day #3. BKnights Promotion (costs $5.00 on Fiverr.com)
Typically, there are readers from Freebooksy that might not check their e-mail right away and I have always had a second day of strong downloads from Freebooksy readers. Most downloads will be in the morning.

Wednesday Day #4. No promotions.

Thursday Day #5 is the day that I decide to end the promotion and do so at 6:30 pm central time. This has the book available in prime time (7:00 to 11:00 pm) on Amazon and I want to have my book converted to paid as soon to prime time as possible.

After stopping the free launch, the book will still would show up in the free rankings for a couple of hours. The book will show a 99-cent price point and it should generate sales for your book. As an example, on this strategy, after the free launch for Positivity Attracts ended, it was #1 in all of its book categories and was in the top 2400 in all of Amazon Kindle once it transitioned back into the paid categories.

With the launches, I want to generate as much buzz as possible and having your book for free for a limited time helps in that process.

While we have touched on some of the marketing in this book, we have not covered everything, as there is a lot of information, especially with marketing your book. In my Book Publishing for Authors Implementation Program, we dedicate two complete modules in the program to my book marketing strategy that will help you implement my own book marketing system that has taken all my books to bestselling status including all my clients.

We cover the exact launch sequence from the day that you upload your book to Amazon, to when to book the promos, including all the current information on who we recommend using. Not only do we take a deep dive into creating your own marketing plan for your book launch, I also include contact information for some of the promo companies including personal email addresses for the bookers of some of the toughest promo sites to get booked on. The information in this chapter will be helpful in your journey, but implementation with the program and me will make a huge difference in the future success of your book.

Chapter 15 Paid Strategy at 99 Cents

Now that you have converted your book to 99 cents it is time to generate traffic to your book and get as many sales as possible. I am following similar concepts from the free strategy with having the book at 99 cents for the next 4.5 days.

Thursday evening. End the free launch around 6:30 pm central time.

Day #1 Friday. No promotions. Amazon will see your book doing well and it will start to be shown in the Customers Who Bought This Item Also Bought section of Kindle Books on Amazon. The publicity gained is great for your book and should help bring in sales.

Day #2 Saturday. Reading Deals promotion. ($29.00)

Day #3 Sunday. Bargain Booksy promotion. ($25.00)

Day #4 Monday. Buck Books promotion. ($35.00)

Day #5 Tuesday. No promotions. Convert your price from 99 cents to either $2.99 or $3.99 at noon central time. If your book is over one-hundred pages then consider $3.99 as a price point.

Sales will slip but remember that your book will be making $2.06 cents per sale instead of .35 cents. Do not worry if things slow down for a day or two. The Amazon Algorithm will kick in and you should see your books being featured in the Customers Also Bought section of many top books. I have seen this for all my books. I checked the Buck Books daily email for the next several days and I saw my books being featured in the Customers Also Bought section every day.

The books that are promoted on Buck Books usually end up in the top 8000 at minimum in Amazon Kindle and I have seen quite a few in the top 2000 including all my books. You will most likely see your book in that section so definitely subscribe to Buck Books for their daily e-mail as it is an efficient way to track your book in that section.

I want to share with you a case study from Mimi Emmanuel. Mimi and I have worked together since early 2016. At the time, Mimi was creating her first book about book publishing. Mimi reached out to me after reading my first publishing book, as she wanted help with her branding, launch and marketing strategy. I helped Mimi with her branding, launch plan and marketing strategy and her book became a bestseller.

Later in 2016 we worked together again on her biggest success yet. Mimi created her second book about book publishing. I helped Mimi again with her branding and launch plan and her book became a bestseller in multiple categories.

The results were amazing. Mimi has published four books that ranked as #1 bestsellers in over forty categories. This is what Mimi said about working with me.

"What I LOVE about Paul is that he 'Walks the Talk.'. He lives what he preaches and delivers on his promises when he helps authors with their branding and publishing their books." Mimi Emmanuel

While we have touched on some of the marketing in this book, we have not covered everything, as there is a lot of information, especially with marketing your book. In my Book Publishing for Authors Implementation Program, we dedicate two complete modules in the program to my book marketing strategy that will help you implement my own book marketing system that has taken all my books to bestselling status including all my clients.

We cover the exact launch sequence from the day that you upload your book to Amazon, to when to book the promos, including all the current information on who we recommend using. Not only do we take a deep dive into creating your own marketing plan for your book launch, I also include contact information for some of the promo companies including personal email address for the bookers of some of the toughest promo sites to get books on. The information in this chapter will be helpful in your journey, but implementation with the program and me will make a huge difference in the future success of your book.

Chapter 16 Recording Your Audiobook

Having multiple revenue streams are critical to becoming not only a successful author, but also in any business. I read an article a couple years ago that explained the average millionaire entrepreneur had an average of seven revenue streams. Audiobooks are another great revenue stream to have as an author.

I decided to add audiobooks to my launches starting with my second book, Motivation 101. With my first book, Eat Less and Move More, I was incredibly busy with the launch and I did not have time to get the audiobook done at the time of the launch. After the launch finished I started to research audiobook options and found that I could do it myself.

When I started recording my own audiobooks, I bought a condenser microphone called the Blue Snowball ICE Condenser Microphone and a pop filter from Amazon. The cost was around $56.00 for both and I downloaded the Audacity program for free, which would allow me to record the book. I used that mic to record seven of my audiobooks.

In 2017, I bought a new microphone. I highly recommend it, the ATR2100-USB Cardioid

Dynamic Microphone. Many authors use this mic to record audiobooks and many podcast hosts use the mic for their podcasts. You can buy the ATR 2100 on Amazon for around sixty-five dollars.

You will also need to reach out to your freelancer and have them convert your Kindle book cover to audiobook size. It should not cost too much and having the cover is just as important for sales as it is for a Kindle cover. Unfortunately, I found this out the hard way. I did not have audiobook covers ready for several weeks after both the Motivation 101 and Eat Less and Move More audiobooks were published. This was a costly mistake not worth repeating.

For Motivation 101, I wanted to have an Audiobook available at the time of the launch for two reasons. The first was to have the additional revenue stream and the second was to use it as a lead magnet.

I recorded the book over two weekends. There is a lot of work that goes into recording it yourself, so you need to decide if you want to take on that responsibility or work a royalty agreement out with having someone else record it for you. I have gone both routes.

As I mentioned earlier in the book, there are three different royalty rates with Audible. If you decide to make the book exclusive to Audible then you will get a forty percent royalty. The royalty percentage does change to twenty percent if you do a royalty share agreement and have a narrator record the audiobook for you. They also will upload the audiobook to Audible for you. The other royalty rate is twenty-five percent and happens when you make the audiobook non-exclusive to Audible. That means that your keep the audiobook rights and can sell it yourself or give it away.

I did that with Motivation 101 and I gave away the audiobook version to add people to my email list. By choosing that route, I added over one thousand subscribers to my email list and was well worth doing.

Over two weekends in 2015, I recorded Motivation 101; it took me two to three hours each weekend to record the audio. It was not an easy process, but I did learn a few things that I will cover.

My first suggestion is to record the smaller chapters first. This also includes the intro, foreword (if you have one), contact information, and some of the smaller chapters. Leave the longer chapters for the following weekend. You will make mistakes and you will have to rerecord chapters again. It is a frustrating process at times, but it does get better.

When I recorded Positivity Attracts, it was much easier and took me four hours instead of five to six hours. I do HIGHLY recommend finding a small room to record in. Do not have the air conditioning or heating on, you want the room as quiet as possible. I also recommend having the mic on at least three to four large hardback books and have the mic six inches from your face. This will help in case your computer fan is a little loud. You will always want to speak into the mic.

Another option is to buy a microphone suspension mic clip adjustable boom studio scissor arm stand. You can find it on Amazon for around twelve dollars. Once you receive the stand all you need to do is use the adjustable mount to mount it to your desk. If you plan to record a lot of audiobooks or online courses, it is perfect, as it will only take you a few seconds to set up for recording.

Once you have recorded a chapter I highly recommend that you listen to it immediately. If it sounds good and you are happy with it, go to the next chapter. Continue the process for those two weekends until your audiobook is complete. I also recommend taking a five to ten-minute break every thirty to forty-five minutes. You will want to get some water and possibly some hot tea, because your vocal chords will get tired. In addition, when recording, you will also want to pause before speaking at the start of each chapter for two to three seconds and then start to speak. At the end of each chapter, also leave two to three seconds of silence.

Once your recording is complete, you will want to send the files to someone who can edit and remaster your recording. In audiobook recordings, ACX wants there to be a slight gap at the beginning and end of each chapter. The two to three seconds of silence is that gap. Your freelancer can make this flow very smoothly, but you do need to leave that space.

For my first book, Eat Less and Move More, I decided that I did not want to record it myself. My other books were around ten thousand words and Eat Less and Move More was almost twice as long. I chose to do a royalty share agreement and had a narrator on ACX do the recording. This option only gives you twenty percent commission as the narrator also gets twenty percent as well. Since I did not want to record it, I felt that twenty percent of something was better than forty percent of nothing.

It is an easy process as you submit the information on ACX and narrators will audition for you. After listening to ten auditions, I chose my narrator and he recorded the book within five days. The narrator also uploads the audiobook to ACX, which is great. It was available on Amazon, Audible, and iTunes within two weeks.

One other thing about ACX is that the audiobook will most likely not be ready in time for your launch. You cannot upload the audiobook until your Kindle eBook is available on Amazon. At that point, you can upload the audiobook. Again, the audiobooks are a long-term investment. You will not make a ton of money starting out and might only make 10-20 dollars on average for the first couple of months. It should pay off long term.

Another great benefit of recording it yourself is that you will find errors in your book that you may not have caught initially. No matter how awesome your editor is (and I have an AMAZING editor) there will be mistakes that do not get caught. Recording the audiobook aloud will help you find the other mistakes. I have found at least ten errors with both Motivation 101 and Positivity Attracts while recording the audiobooks.

If you are going to record an audiobook yourself, I would recommend recording the audiobook first before having your book converted to Kindle. For my books, I use the Microsoft Word version of my book to record the audiobooks and then made corrections to any errors found to the file while recording the audiobook; I have the final draft converted to Kindle and then paperback. I will be covering the paperback process in our next chapter.

Before we move to the next chapter I want to share the feedback that I received from one of my students that is currently in the Book Publishing for Authors Implementation program. I am sharing her feedback in this chapter as one of Hillary's goals as an author is to record and narrate her audiobooks.

"I read Paul Brodie's book, Book Publishing for Beginners, and his style of writing immediately put me at ease. He not only provided well-thought out step-by-step instructions, insights, and behind-the-scenes knowledge about self-publishing that only someone with his experience and expertise could know, but he shared them with encouragement and a 'you can do

this' attitude. Because of Paul's in-depth knowledge and positive attitude when I realized I needed a real-life coach to show me how to market my books and create audiobooks, I signed up for his Book Publishing for Authors Implementation Program. It was the best decision! With Paul by my side, I'm no longer afraid to record my first audiobook, and I know my books will get into the hands of my readers." Hillary Tubin, Author of Boys and Books

Chapter 17 Converting Your Book to Paperback

Once you have recorded your audiobook and corrected any final errors to your book (most likely in a Microsoft Word file) to send to your freelancer for Kindle MOBI conversion then it is time to convert your book to paperback.

Converting your word file to paperback for CreateSpace is something that you can do yourself. It will take you anywhere from thirty minutes to two hours to convert the book. I have found a great resource that you can watch to convert the book yourself free.

There is a great tutorial on YouTube by author India Drummond. All you need to do is type her name into the YouTube search bar to find it. The process will take you through how to convert your draft to CreateSpace. As part of the Book Publishing for Authors Implementation Program, my student authors receive the systematic guide on how to convert the book that is based off the tutorial. The only cost out of your pocket for the conversion will be for the paperback book cover (usually around $25.00 on Fiverr). CreateSpace will provide a free ISBN number or you can buy one from them if you prefer.

For the book cover, I would recommend using the same freelancer that you use for your Kindle cover. My freelancer charges me $25.00, which I feel is a great value. You will need to decide what you want on the back of the book cover. I feel it's a good idea to have your book description (also known as your sales copy) for your Kindle book on the back of the paperback cover.

Send that information to your freelancer so they can add it to your back cover. Another thing is that if you use your sales copy, make sure you take out any parts like "buy this now" at the top of the page. I made that mistake in the paperback book cover for Positivity Attracts and had to have my freelancer make the edits after the cover was already completed.

It will take a few days to get the book cover back from your freelancer, as it is more work compared to the Kindle cover. Once you get the cover and the ISBN, and have the conversion ready (don't forget to convert your converted CreateSpace ready word file to PDF) and then you can upload to CreateSpace.

You will also need to place the book in a book category on CreateSpace and it doesn't have to be the same as you chose on Kindle. You can choose something different if you would like. The categories will be a little different, so you might not be able to choose the same exact category anyway.

One final item that you will need to decide on is how much you want to charge for your book. All my books are priced at $9.99, and I have found that to be a good price point. My commission on that price point is $3.84 per book sold. At that point, you will be able to get the book uploaded.

One of the best things about CreateSpace is that it works very quickly. Similar to ACX, you must have your Kindle eBook uploaded to Amazon and it must be live. Your CreateSpace book should be available on Amazon within 3-4 days.

In my view, having the book available as both paperback and Kindle creates several advantages. The first one is that you have several options for readers from which to choose. There are people that do not read Kindle books, but do want paperback books. Having the paperback book will entice the reader who does not use Kindle to buy your book. The other part is perceived value.

The reader sees two prices when they go to your book page on Amazon. They will notice the print edition for $9.99 and in contrast will see your Kindle book for only $2.99. It is even better when your book is listed at free or 99 cents as it will also show how much you save with the Kindle edition. It will show 70 percent off when priced at $2.99 and 90 percent off at 99 cents.

I did not have a paperback edition of Eat Less and Move More ready until mid-September. However, I did notice when converting the book that I had a few errors in the Kindle version from my initial word file. I had my freelancer who does my Kindle conversions make a quick update so that I could have the errors fixed which were not caught at the initial launch.

With having paperback versions of both Motivation 101 and Positivity Attracts available when the books launched, I did see increased sales and at minimum I recommend having both paperback and Kindle versions available for when you launch.

All my books from Motivation 101 onwards have all had three formats ready for each book launch through Kindle, paperback, and audiobook. By having all three available, you will be able to maximize revenue on the front-end of your book launch.

Chapter 18 How to Build Your Audience

Now it is time to begin building your audience if you have not already done so. When you release your book, you will have traffic coming to it. Your Kindle will have traffic from Amazon, your audiobook traffic will come from Amazon and Audible, and your paperback traffic will come from Amazon and CreateSpace. Your goal is to funnel as much of that traffic as possible to your list to build your own audience.

When I first heard the term funnel I was not clear on what it meant. The goal of the term funnel is to move the readers who buy your books on Amazon, Audible, and CreateSpace to your email list.

Your goal is to funnel as many readers of your books as possible to your email list. That way, you can contact them yourself since Amazon is not going to give you the names of the readers who buy your books. The best way to get the readers funneled to your list is to give them something of value through having a lead magnet.

MailChimp is the list service that I currently use. It is free for your first two thousand subscribers. After you reach two thousand subscribers, you must pay for the service. MailChimp is good, but they do not offer an auto responder option for the free service. An auto responder is where you can draft a series of email messages over a span of time that a new subscriber to your list will receive when they sign up to your list. Originally, I was going to change my email provider from Mailchimp to AWeber once I went over two thousand subscribers, but decided to stay with Mailchimp.

As a new author starting out, I highly recommend starting with Mailchimp as it does take time to build your email list. It took me eighteen months to get over two thousand subscribers. Going with Mailchimp to get started is a great option, especially while the service is free for the first two thousand subscribers.

Once you get over two thousand subscribers I would recommend looking at several services. AWeber and Infusionsoft are two email providers worth looking at. You also might want to look at ClickFunnels. Their premium package is expensive at two hundred ninety-seven dollars per month, but that is for an unlimited number of subscribers.

With Mailchimp, AWeber, and Infusionsoft you will pay more per month as your list grows. That is why I highly recommend using Mailchimp while getting started.

Another benefit of Mailchimp is that it is easy to use, has a high delivery rate and will reach your readers. Sometimes AWeber and Infusionsoft have challenges at times with delivering emails. It doesn't happen often from what I have heard from other authors, but things do happen. Mailchimp is a lot more reliable and is one of the main reasons that I continue to use the service, even though I now pay a monthly fee.

Another thing you will want to create is your own website. It does not have to be fancy although you can make it look good for an inexpensive price. The goal of your website is to have a site where readers can reach you and get your lead magnets.

You can get webhosting for as little as three dollars and ninety-five cents per month through Bluehost for a three-year agreement. The catch is that you do have to pay in advance, but that price point is well worth the investment.

The only other item you will need to buy regarding the hosting side of your site is to buy the domain. You should be able to purchase the domain for between six to twelve dollars per year. Bluehost offers phone support and they can walk you through the set-up process. Recently I set up a website for my dad from scratch and they walked me through the process in less than twenty minutes.

The only other item you will need to purchase is a premium WordPress theme. Recently I purchased a premium theme called The7 – Responsive Multi-Purpose WordPress Theme. The theme cost me forty dollars and it was a significant upgrade over my previous website design, which was a free theme from WordPress.

Once you purchase the theme (or any premium) theme you can contact Bluehost and they can walk you through the process. It is a straightforward process and is easier than you think. If you are not comfortable with creating the website yourself, you do have an option to have Bluehost build your site for you. It is whatever you prefer, but I would recommend trying to build the site yourself if you feel comfortable with trying it.

You have some additional options for building your website as you can also hire freelancers on Fiverr or Upwork to build the site for you. In terms of price, the costs would be similar to having Bluehost build it for you. You can also reach out to other authors to see how they built their sites and who they used.

When I started my website, I had a friend build it for me. A basic WordPress theme that looked nice while getting started. I have used the site for the past two years and took over the maintenance of the site with updates and additions to it in 2016. It was through maintaining the site myself where I learned more about WordPress and became comfortable with how it works. I learned how to manage the various plugins and how to make changes to the website including how to purchase and install premium WordPress themes to make my website look even better.

Once you have decided on your email service and website it is time to think about how you are going to build your audience, otherwise known as your subscribers. Your subscriber list is your tribe so to speak. Your subscribers on your list have a connection to you through your book and are interested in what you are offering. Building a large reader list is critical to an author's success and to their revenue streams.

Chapter 19 Lead Magnets

The first thing you need to do is decide on what type of lead magnet that you want to give away. Lead magnets are what you will be giving away to your reader to get them to join your list. In this chapter, I am going to tell you about two companies I use for my lead magnets.

I use Lead Pages (costs thirty-seven dollars per month for the standard plan) to offer freebies to get readers. For that price, you get virtually unlimited pages that you can create. You also do not need your own website as lead pages host the pages on their page. Lead Pages currently offers a 14-day free trial.

If you do have your own website, you can redirect the page to your website. For example, my free Motivation 101 audiobook is hosted on Lead Pages but is also available at www.BrodieEDU.com/freeaudiobook.

I would suggest Lead Pages if you are starting out as the lower cost might be a better option compared to ClickFunnels. Earlier in 2017, I added ClickFunnels due to wanting to accept secure online payments. The service is more expensive, but they do offer the best landing pages around and the easiest to create. You can create a landing page in less than a minute. ClickFunnels costs ninety-seven dollars a month, but with the secure payment option was worth the upgrade.

Both Lead Pages and ClickFunnels offer options to create links on your own website through WordPress plugins and are easy to install. It looks better having the landing pages link to your own website and are easier to promote in your books and through external links that you can share on social media through Facebook, Twitter, and Instagram.

ClickFunnels currently has a 14-day free trial. The lead pages funnels and payment forms are easy to create. If you are looking to create payment forms for offers including coaching programs and online training then I highly recommend starting with ClickFunnels.

My first freebie was created for the launch of my first book, Eat Less and Move More in August 2015. I wrote both Eat Less and Move More and version 1 of my second book, Motivation 101. Version 1 of Motivation 101 had my old cover that I wrote about earlier in the book and was edited, but was not a final copy.

It was a great lead magnet as I got over 100 readers to sign up to my list. In September 2015, I edited the lead page and changed out the free book of Motivation 101 to the free audiobook. I finalized Motivation 101 with a new cover and a final round of edits and launched the eBook on Amazon in mid-September for an early October launch.

The audiobook of Motivation 101 was my new lead magnet and did well. Since adding the audiobook as a lead magnet, we have added over one-thousand subscribers to my email list through giving away the audiobook.

A strategy that I have learned from Kevin Kruse, is to make offers for each chapter of a book. You identify a theme in the chapter and offer something that correlates, and then have all the items in one bundle. You will notice that strategy in this book with offering free access to my Get Published Facebook Community. What I realized is that there was a lot of additional information that I felt could be covered in the Facebook group and would be another great place to connect.

Having multiple offers in a book (like this one) greatly increases the probability of funneling the reader to your list. One of my most important goals is not only to build a great list of readers, but also to always give people a lot of value free. At times, I will offer a service, such as my free Get Published Webinar, but the main things I will be offering is freebies and free advanced copies of my books. That way, there is always value for the readers as I hope that many of you will take advantage of one of the offers in this book. The free Get Published training is also offered at the beginning of this book.

If you do want to know what item has brought me the most subscribers it is by far the audiobook giveaway. The Motivation 101 audiobook has added over one-thousand subscribers to my list and that number has grown every day. Another thing to look at is the statistics that both Lead Pages and ClickFunnels offer for their landing pages.

The statistics will show your conversion rate. Your conversion rate is the percent of people that go to your page and download your offer. Typically, any conversion rate over thirty percent is good.

I have given away a variety of items in my books ranging from travel guides (thirty-four percent conversion), to an author resource guide (forty-two percent conversion) to motivational guides (conversion rate of thirty three percent on average).

My Motivation 101 audiobook conversion rate is forty-three percent and is a great conversion rate. Audiobooks are also very popular and is a great way to promote back-end offerings that we will cover in the next chapter as several of my clients contacted me initially after listening to the audiobook version of one of my books.

You can also offer sneak previews of your upcoming books by offering the first chapter. Another option is to record the first chapter of your next book in audiobook format and offer that as a lead magnet.

Chapter 20 Back-End Products

Back-end products are going to be where you make the most revenue from your book launch. It is the reason why you want to funnel traffic from Amazon by building your audience through your subscriber email list. This is also why we want to get your book into the hands of as many people as possible and is why I highly recommend giving your book away for free for part of your book launch.

The whole point of building your list is to be able to not only give value to your readers, but also to offer products and services otherwise known as back-end products. I offer several services including Done for You Packages ranging from publishing your book to running your entire book launch to One-On-One coaching to a limited number of clients for a three-month period.

My main offer is my Book Publishing for Authors Implementation Program. The program includes ten video modules and five live group video coaching calls with me and was created over the summer of 2017. The implementation program is the ideal system if you want to publish and market your book to a #1 bestseller.

The program is offered at the end of my free Get Published Webinar Training. In the webinar, I teach a lot of great content that helps people publish and market their book regardless of whether they decide to join my program.

I have always believed in offering the best content possible and in the training, we teach amazing content for the first forty-five minutes. In the final fifteen minutes, I go over the offer as we do offer a significant discount for anyone who joins the program during the webinar.

The Book Publishing for Authors Implementation Program is amazing. It includes ten video modules covering the entire book publishing process from finishing your book, finding the best book cover, how to get reviews, my entire book marketing system and is the same exact system that I have used to launch all my books to bestselling status and also all of my clients, how to maximize revenue streams on the front-end with how to have your book available in Kindle, Paperback, and Audiobook formats for your launch (including how-to guides), how to build your audience, how to offer back-end products to maximize revenue from public speaking, online courses, and coaching.

In the program, we take a deep dive into each area of book publishing and the weekly modules average between thirty-five to fifty-five minutes for each module. The modules are sent out on a weekly basis for ten weeks and you also get two bonus modules including several additional bonuses from joining our Book Publishing for Authors secret Facebook group, free products from this book including an autographed paperback copy, a free sixty minute One-On-One strategy session with me and several other bonuses. With the program, the most important part is that it isn't done for you or do it yourself. It is done with you as we implement together and that is the secret sauce when you choose to work with me.

I also offer motivational speaking and have an offer in the front matter of each of my seminar series books. Originally, my goal as an author was to increase business with my motivational speaking services and it made a significant difference where I can now charge $2,500-$5,000 depending on the event. I mainly speak at college campuses, but our corporate business has also increased. Those increases have happened due to offering additional seminars that expanded from motivational seminars to leadership seminars.

Offering public speaking is a great way to expand your business. Having a paperback version of your book will make all the difference in increasing your public speaking business. Your book will make you an authority in your area of expertise. I give away paperback versions of my book during seminars as lead magnets in return for having audience members fill out interest forms to bring me to their campus or business. It works as I typically have at least fifteen to twenty-five leads at the end of every seminar that I receive through giving away the paperback book, which is typically the book version of the seminar.

I want to share with you a case study from Bradley Miles. Bradley reached out to me in early 2017 after listening to the audiobook version of my first publishing book. He needed help with the revenue stream part of his book launch with both having a paperback version of his book and how to position the book into speaking opportunities.

We came up with a game plan to make Bradley an authority in Venture Capital through his book, #Break Into VC. Bradley also requested my help with his branding, launch plan and marketing strategy. We set a very specific marketing strategy, which both the free launch and 99-cent launch before the price increased to the regular price. The book was also available in paperback so he could sell them through CreateSpace and purchase copies directly from CreateSpace to give away at his speaking events.

The results were amazing as Bradley had his first bestselling book one month after graduating from college. He makes significant revenue on the back-end from speaking engagements across the United States thanks to the success of his book. This is what Bradley had to say about working with me.

"I was a student with a dream of writing and one day becoming a bestselling author. It seemed like a dream a lifetime away, but after learning from Paul, I understood the importance of writing what I know and how to achieve bestseller status on Amazon.

After writing about my journey towards a career in venture capital, my book #BreakIntoVC turned into a bestseller in the venture capital category and has created a tremendous amount of opportunities for me.

Since writing my book I have lectured at Harvard, Wharton, Columbia, USC and many other schools. Paul's advice about book publishing and the power of multiple revenue streams are invaluable and I owe a lot to Paul's coaching." Bradley Miles

Becoming a Book Publishing Coach in early 2016 has made me a considerable amount of revenue for me on the back-end and the coaching combined with my motivational speaking events enabled me to leave my job as a Special Education Teacher in June 2017. This was achieved while teaching full-time, so there is time to build a business for you and a catalog of back-end products that you can offer to your readership while still working full-time.

One thing I want to make clear about coaching is that you need to decide on the niche that you want to coach in if you have not already done so. Different niches include life coaching, health and wellness, spirituality, travel, real estate, helping people relocate to a new area, or book publishing.

You do not want to make your coaching too general. You want it to be specific to be successful.

Webinars are another great way to promote your product or service. I will freely admit that I completely screwed up my first webinar product. I created a lead page and promoted it actively in the release of Motivation 101. I was selling a three-part webinar for $49.99 (50 percent off the $99.99 price point). It would address three key components from the book with the first one covering Our Greatest Opponent. It failed miserably!

What I should have done was offer a FREE webinar and then sold my coaching service on the back-end. I would have most likely made a lot more revenue with that initial webinar and it was a lesson learned. Sometimes products will sell well, and sometimes they will fail.

Another back-end product that is worth considering is creating video courses. Creating an online course is a way for you to create content and have students sign up. It does take a lot of work to set up, but it is a great opportunity to make significant passive income as once your product is uploaded then you market it and start to build your business. My goal is to create multiple smaller courses with courses including how to create your own audiobook, how to become a professional speaker, and other courses.

All you need to do is purchase an account on Vimeo.com where you can upload up to five gigs of data per week. The initial account to get started costs sixty dollars per year and a business account costs twenty dollars per month. I recently upgraded my account to a business account due to the growth of my Book Publishing for Authors Implementation Program.

To record the content, you can use the microphone that I recommended earlier in this book and buy video capture software. I use Debut Video Capture Software. It cost me twenty-five dollars for the license and the instructions are easy to follow. To create an online course, you can create between six to ten video modules. You can create power point slides through Microsoft Word or use Open Office for each module. Once the slides are created, you can use Debut to record your narration for the module. Use the information that you create in the slides and then expand on the information when recording the narration.

The potential with online courses is to make hundreds if not thousands of dollars a month, but it does take time. The best advice I can give to any author is to be patient. This is a marathon, not a sprint. It is a process and it takes time.

Rome was not built in a day and it does take patience as you slowly build your back-end offerings. Therefore, I want you to be clear on what you want to get out of publishing your own book. Is it the opportunity to do public speaking? Is it to begin or expand your professional coaching? Do you want to create an online course?

Chapter 21 Revenue Streams

In previous chapters, I have mentioned having multiple revenue streams. This is the key to becoming successful in any business and especially as an author. Having just a Kindle version of your book in my view is not enough, especially with starting out. At minimum, I highly recommend having both a Kindle and paperback version of your book ready for each book launch. Below are potential revenue streams.

Kindle Edition of your book

Paperback Edition (Createspace)

Audiobook (ACX)

Public Speaking

Coaching

Book Signings

Online Courses

The paperback edition of your book is essentially the modern-day business card. It is a great way to promote yourself and I highly recommend always having several copies of each of your books with you, either in your car or in your backpack, purse, etc. I also recommend reaching out to bookstores where you live to see about book signings. They are a great potential revenue stream. You can typically buy your books from CreateSpace in bulk (around 100 copies) for around $250.00 to $300.00. If you end up selling 100 books at a book signing then your profit margin is potentially $700.00 on one successful book signing.

One thing that I do is have book signings at the end of my motivational seminars when speaking at university campuses or for companies. I will offer either a package deal ($1000.00 for 100 books to sign) or sell them ala cart. It is a great way to bring in additional revenue and the investment is well worth it.

There are many revenue streams to utilize. These are a few helpful ideas on your journey to becoming a bestselling author.

Chapter 22 Summary: The Book Publishing Journey

We have covered a lot of information in this book. By the time you have made it to this chapter (unless you skipped ahead to read the summary) you have read over twenty-five thousand words. This is the longest book I have written and the scary part is that we have only scratched the surface of book publishing.

I want to share with you a testimonial from one of my student authors in the Book Publishing for Authors Implementation Program. Shawn is an entrepreneur and is in his early twenties. He is writing his first book currently and is running it like a business.

"Paul's Book Publishing for Authors Implementation Program is a winner on so many fronts. It beautifully and easily synthesizes the publishing process. The program is perfect for any experience level: the author just starting out without a lick of experience with publishing, Kindle, or eCommerce all the way to the seasoned bestselling veteran author who wants to take their publishing to the next level." Shawn Richardson

There are many moving parts when it comes to writing, publishing and launching your book, especially if you want your book to become a #1 bestseller. One question I get often is what exactly is a #1 bestseller?

Having a #1 bestseller is when your book is number one in at least one book category. You see that information in the subtitle of this book as I mention the outcome of a number one bestseller. It doesn't matter if your book is a bestseller for an hour or six months, the moment you see that your book is number one in its category then your book is a bestseller.

The point is that your book peaked as a bestseller on Amazon and thus you are officially a bestselling author. It is harder than it seems, but by reading this book, joining our Get Published Facebook Community, and watching your complementary Get Published Training you will be in a much better position to succeed.

Throughout the book we have covered the beginning of the journey, advice from other bestselling authors, getting you clear on why you are writing your book, idea topics for your book, choosing your book title, and outlining and writing your book.

Once your book is written we covered the editing process, how to get your book formatted, choosing a great book cover, creating your book description to help sell your book, and how to upload your book, and getting reviews.

We covered a brief overview of both the free and ninety-nine cent book launch strategy, how to record your audiobook, the conversion process to paperback, how to build your audience, lead magnets, back-end offers, and revenue streams.

One thing I want to make clear is that no one can do it themselves. We all need help! I am a huge believer in having help and I hired a business coach earlier this year myself. It was the best decision I ever made with hiring my coach and going through his program. The money I invested in the program was significant, but I have already made many times the amount back due to what I learned in his program. It was life changing when I decided to hire a coach to help me implement. Best part is that the investment often is tax deductible. Check with your countries tax laws, but I was able to write off the investment of hiring my own coach on my taxes.

After graduating from the initial program, I met with my coach at his workshop in Santa Monica,

California in early October. We spoke about the future and I applied to join his mastermind program called Black Belt. It was a significant investment and the membership was twenty thousand dollars for the next twelve months. After having a follow-up call I was invited to join Black Belt and I accepted. I mention this because having the right mentality is key when you are ready to make serious changes and improvement in your life. The main thing to look for is what will the outcome be? I already know that my outcome with the return on investment will be significant because of the focus, accountability, and implementation that comes with Taki's Black Belt program.

Having a coach brings focus, accountability, and implementation to getting your book created, published and marketed. It also will help build your business quickly with a proven system that works. The hardest part about publishing and marketing your book is the implementation process, which is the primary benefit you will get should we end up working together.

I want to share with you one final testimonial from a current student in the Book Publishing for Authors Implementation Program. Liza is writing her first book currently and it is a guidebook about Maui, a place near and dear to my heart. This is what Liza had to say about working with me and the program.

"Paul Brodie's Book Publishing for Authors Implementation Program is the key that unlocked my writing and publishing dream and is helping make it a reality. I have been wanting to write and publish a guidebook for Maui, but was overwhelmed by the all the things I needed to learn and the many steps needed to make it happen. However, Paul's program and coaching broke down the overwhelming task to simplified doable weekly tasks. The detailed step-by-step system in addition to the live group coaching calls with Paul has enabled me to make significant progress to actually accomplish the steps towards making my writing and publishing dream come true." Liza Pierce

One of the most important questions that you need to ask yourself is this.

What are you willing to invest to change your life?

If you are reading this book then you are most likely at a fork in the road. You want to make a change.

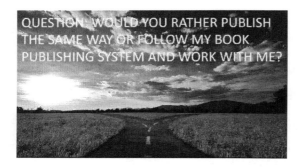

The change you want to make involves either expanding your business or starting a new business. If you are a business owner, having a book is essential to build and expand your business. It also most likely involves the goal to leave your current job eventually, especially if you are working for someone else. I know that because that is the situation for most of my clients, and student authors in my Book Publishing for Authors Implementation Program, which offers the ideal system if you are wanting to publish and market your book to a #1 bestseller.

I was also in that same situation two years ago when I wrote, published, and marketed my first book. At that time, I was making good money teaching, but I was not making a lot of additional income. After that trip to Las Vegas I started to write my first book. Once the book was written, I realized that I needed more money to be able to pay for my first launch while waiting for the royalties to come in. Once your book is launched, it takes two months to get your first royalty check from Amazon.

I knew that I would be spending at least a couple thousand dollars with publishing and marketing my first book. Once I realized the investment that was necessary, I made the decision to ask my dad for a loan. I told him my business plan and he lent me two thousand dollars so I could get the book published and marketed properly.

That loan resulted in starting a business that now makes significant revenue two years later with multiple revenue streams on the front-end with each of my books releases in Kindle, audiobook, and paperback and on the back-end with speaking events, One-On-One coaching, Done for You publishing and marketing packages, and my Book Publishing for Authors Implementation Program.

Taking that risk two years ago and taking the plunge enabled me to leave my job as a teacher, be my own boss, and set my own hours. The commute is now ten seconds from the living room to my home office and I love it. The best part is working with others to help them write, publish and market their books to bestselling status and more importantly helping them change their lives.

Every one of my clients has become a bestseller and I take a lot of pride in that. I strongly recommend investing your time by reading this book, joining our Get Published Facebook Community, and watching your complementary Get Published Training Webinar.

I would love to work with you either through having you join the Book Publishing for Authors Implementation Program, One-On-One Coaching, or by publishing and marketing your book for you.

Now it is time for you to decide and answer the following question one more time.

What are you willing to invest to change your life?

Please spread the word about this book and the implementation program with your friends if they are also looking to change their lives. If there is anything I can do for you then please let me know.

Thank you for investing your time in reading my book and I look forward to hearing about your future success.

Go to www.BrodieEDU.com and click on the Free Webinar tab to watch your complementary Get Published Training

More Books by Paul

"Quick and inexpensive reads for self-improvement, a healthier lifestyle, and book publishing"

Nine-time Amazon bestselling author, Paul Brodie believes that books should be inexpensive, straightforward, direct, and not have a bunch of fluff.

Each of his books were created to solve problems including living a healthy lifestyle, increasing motivation, improving positive thinking, traveling to amazing destinations, and helping authors write, publish and market their books to a #1 bestseller.

What makes Paul's books different is his ability to explain complex ideas and strategies in a simple, accessible way that you can implement immediately.

Want to know more?

Go to www.BrodieEDU.com/Books

About the Author

Paul Brodie is the President of BrodieEDU, an education consulting firm that specializes in giving motivational, business, publishing, and leadership seminars for universities and corporations. He is also the CEO of Brodie Consulting Group, which specializes in book publishing and coaching clients on how to publish and market their books.

Brodie recently left teaching after serving as an educator in multiple roles since 2008. He served as a Special Education Teacher from 2014-2017 in the Hurst-Euless-Bedford ISD (2014-2016) and Fort Worth ISD (2016-2017) while working specifically with special needs children who had Autism. In 2014-2015 he also served as the head tennis coach and lead the school to a district championship and an undefeated season.

From 2011-2014, Brodie served as a Grant Coordinator for the ASPIRE program in the Birdville Independent School District. As coordinator, he created instructional and enrichment programming for over 800 students and 100 parents in the ASPIRE before and after school programs. He also served on the Board of Directors for the Leadership Development Council, Inc. from 2005-2014 with leading the implementation of educational programming in low cost housing.

From 2008-2011, he was a highly successful teacher in Arlington, TX where he taught English as a Second Language. Brodie turned a once struggling ESL program into one of the top programs in the school district. Many of his students moved on to journalism, AVID, art classes, and many students exited the ESL program entirely.

Teaching methods during his career as an educator included daily writing practice, flash cards, picture cards, academic relays, music, movies, and short educational videos including the alphabet and sight words. Additional strategies included graphic novels paired with movie versions of the novels, games, cultural celebrations, and getting parents involved in their children's education. Brodie's approach has been called unconventional but very effective, revolutionary, and highly engaging. His students have always shown great improvement with both academics and behavior throughout the school year and he was honored to teach such an amazing and diverse group of students during his career as an educator.

Previously, Brodie spent many years in the corporate world and decided to leave a lucrative career in the medical field to follow his passion and transitioned into education. Prior to working in the medical field, he worked for Enterprise Rent-A-Car after receiving his Bachelor's Degree and for Savitz Research during his high school and college years. He is very grateful for every career opportunity as each one was an avenue to learn and grow.

Brodie earned an M.A. in Teaching from Louisiana College and B.B.A. in Management from the University of Texas at Arlington. Brodie is a bestselling author and has written multiple books. He wrote his first book, Eat Less and Move More: My Journey in the summer of 2015. Brodie's goal of the book was to help those like himself who had challenges with weight. The goal of his first book was to promote not only weight loss but also health and wellness. He is also the author of Motivation 101, Positivity Attracts, Book Publishing for Beginners, The Pursuit of Happiness, Maui, Just Do It, PMA and San Diego. All nine books (available in Kindle, Paperback, and Audiobook) are Amazon bestsellers and are based on his motivational seminars, book publishing, love of travel, and struggles with weight.

His seminars have been featured at many universities and at leadership conferences across the United States since 2005. Brodie is active in professional organizations and within the community and currently serves on the Advisory Board for Advent Urban Youth Development and as a volunteer with the Special Olympics. He continues to be involved with The International

Business Fraternity of Delta Sigma Pi and has served in many positions since 2002 including National Vice President – Organizational Development, Leadership Foundation Trustee, National Organizational Development Chair, District Director, and in many other volunteer leadership roles. He resides in Arlington, TX.

Testimonials

"Questions that I am frequently asked are, How did you do it? and How can I write and publish my own book? I'm fortunate in that I can now answer these questions in part by referring people to Paul Brodie.

Paul offers very specific advice without the fluff, based on his own journey as a multi-time bestselling author. I've seen how Paul's momentum and success has grown with every new book he's released.

Not everybody can become a $100,000 author; not everyone even wants to be a six-figure author. But if you are looking to get in the book publishing game, Paul's coaching and publishing services can get you from first draft through a successful launch."

Kevin Kruse, Multi-time Bestselling Author and CEO of LEADx

"Paul Brodie is a leader in the field of self-publishing. With his step-by-step publishing and writing strategies and attention to detail during the book launch, he has

provided me with a rock-solid system for writing, publishing and launching a series of bestsellers."

Scott Allan, Multi-time Bestselling Author

"Paul's the real deal! His books and workshops are very down to earth, and he's not afraid to tell you the harsh truth when it's needed. I also really appreciate his willingness to be vulnerable, and share the struggles he's been through, and what he did to move on from there. He's a great guy whose genuine interest to help others is empowering and contagious."

Barry Watson, Bestselling Author of Sell With Confidence

"I have no hesitation in recommending Paul's coaching programs. Paul has a great way of distilling complex information into a form that allows you to quickly understand and absorb the information.

Where Paul excels, though, is in supporting authors in their journey to get published. He not only shows you what you need to do, but provides you with next action steps and when you need them, so you're not overwhelmed and can just focus on what you need to get done next.

Paul is friendly, knows what he is talking about and will get you where you need to be on your self-publishing journey."

Lise Cartwright, Multi-time Bestselling Author and Founder of Hustle and Groove

"With multiple bestsellers under his belt, Paul Brodie is the ideal person to coach others from initial idea to bestseller. His books and workshops provide a step-by-step path to success at self-publishing and he really cares about helping others succeed. Paul makes the very complicated process of writing and publishing easy and fun."

Davina Chessid, Bestselling Author of Food Crazy Mind

Acknowledgments

Thank you to God for guidance and protection throughout my life.

Thank YOU, the reader, for investing your time reading this book.

Thank you to my amazing mom, Barbara Brodie for all the years of support and a kick in the butt when needed.

Thank you to my awesome sister, Dr. Heather Ottaway for all the help and feedback with my books and with my motivational seminars. It is scary how similar we are.

Thank you to Devin Mooneyham for serving as the editor of my tenth book. The slicing and dicing as always was very much appreciated and I could not have gotten this book published without her assistance.

Thank you to Mimi Emmanuel, Scott Allan, and Lise Cartwright for writing forwards for this book.

Thank you to all the authors who contributed to the author advice chapter.

Thank you to Lindsay Palmer who is working tirelessly to get me booked on college campuses for seminars throughout the United States. I could not have a better team of people to work with on Team Brodie.

Thank you to all who have served on the BrodieEDU Advisory Board.

Thank you to my dad, Bill "The Wild Scotsman" Brodie for his encouragement and support with the business aspects of BrodieEDU and Brodie Consulting Group.

Thank you to Shannon and Robert Winckel (two members of the four horsemen with myself and our good friend, Derrada Rubell-Asbell) for their friendship and support. Shannon and Robert are two of my best teacher friends and are always great sounding boards for ideas.

Thank you to (Don) Omar Sandoval for his friendship and help with several BrodieEDU projects including building our awesome website.

Thank you to all the amazing friends that I have worked with over the past twenty plus years. Each of them has made a great impact on my life.

Thank you to all my students that I have had the honor to teach over the years. I am very proud of each of my kids.

Thank you to Delta Sigma Pi Business Fraternity. I learned a great deal about public speaking and leadership through the organization and every experience that I have had helped me become the person that I am today.

Thank you to my three best friends: J. Dean Craig, Jen Mamber, and Aaron Krzycki. We have gone through a lot together and I look forward to many more years of friendship.

Thank you to all the students past and present at the UT Arlington and UT Austin chapters of DSP. Both schools mean a lot to me and I look forward to seeing them again at some point soon.

Thank you to the Lott Family (Stacy, Kerry, Lexi, and Austin) for their friendship over the past seven years.

Thank you to Robin Clites for always taking care of things at the house with ensuring that Mom and I can always get that family vacation every year.

Contact Information

Go to www.BrodieEDU.com/seminars to see why you should consider booking Paul for your campus or organization.

Paul can be reached at Brodie@BrodieConsultingGroup.com

Website www.BrodieEDU.com

@BrodieEDU on Twitter

Paul G. Brodie author page on Facebook

Paul G. Brodie author page on Amazon

BrodieEDU Facebook Page

BrodieEDU YouTube Channel

Feedback Request

Please leave a review for my book as I would greatly appreciate your feedback.

I also welcome you to contact me with any suggestions at Brodie@BrodieConsultingGroup.com

Made in the USA
Columbia, SC
06 November 2017